Sacred Earth,
Sacred Soul

SACRED EARTH, SACRED SOUL

CELTIC WISDOM FOR REAWAKENING
TO WHAT OUR SOULS KNOW AND HEALING THE WORLD

JOHN PHILIP NEWELL

HarperOne
An Imprint of HarperCollins*Publishers*

SACRED EARTH, SACRED SOUL. Copyright © 2021 by John Philip Newell. All rights reserved. Printed in the United States of America. No part of this book may be used or reproduced in any manner whatsoever without written permission except in the case of brief quotations embodied in critical articles and reviews. For information, address HarperCollins Publishers, 195 Broadway, New York, NY 10007.

HarperCollins books may be purchased for educational, business, or sales promotional use. For information, please email the Special Markets Department at SPsales@harpercollins.com.

FIRST EDITION

Designed by Kyle O'Brien
Art by artdock / Shutterstock, Inc.

Library of Congress Cataloging-in-Publication Data is available upon request.

ISBN 978-0-06-302349-9

22 23 24 25   LSC · 10 9 8 7 6 5 4

To
Ember, Santino, and Lena Rumi
and all the grandchildren of the world
that they may inherit the earth
and live in love with her

CONTENTS

INTRODUCTION

We know things in the core of our being that we have not necessarily been taught, and some of this deep knowing may actually be at odds with what our society or religion has tried to teach us. This book is about reawakening to what we know in the depths of our being, that the earth is sacred and that this sacredness is at the heart of every human being and life-form. To awaken again to this deep knowing is to be transformed in the ways we choose to live and relate and act.

The idea that what is deepest in us corresponds to what is true is not a new concept. From the ancient Greek philosopher Plato to the twentieth-century founder of analytical psychology, C. G. Jung, and many others in between, it has been argued that for us to recognize truth, there must be something within us that already knows it. And, most important, we have all experienced this correlation within ourselves and witnessed it in others.

Why was there such concern around the world during the Australian fires of 2019 when millions of creatures were dying in the blaze? Why did the #MeToo movement take off so quickly in recent years in which hundreds of thousands of women came forward to speak out against abuse? Why did the Black Lives Matter protests burst onto the international stage within days of the murder of George Floyd in Minneapolis? In each of these situations, deep down, we knew something sacred was at stake. And we woke up.

The problem is that we keep going back to sleep, or otherwise live in ways that neglect this deep knowing. Thus, the crises that we are in the midst of today, whether ecological, political, or societal, stem from the fact that we treat the earth and one another as less than sacred. All these critical issues are interrelated. The way we have wronged the earth is the way we have dishonored the feminine or belittled the "other," whether that is the "other" nation, religion, race, or sexual orientation. We have fallen out of alignment with the deepest truths within us. How are we to awaken again to the sacredness at the heart of all life, the sacredness that is also at the heart of our own being?

The Celtic spiritual tradition is one that has long emphasized an awareness of the sacred essence of all things. This tradition is in fact part of our Western Christian inheritance, although it has been largely forgotten and at times suppressed. It is this lost stream of wisdom that I will be drawing on in these pages to help us remember. It is a way of seeing, a path of awareness, that can be traced through the centuries, forever unfolding, evolving, emerging again and again to serve a consciousness of the sacred at the heart of all life.

What is unique about the Celtic tradition compared to most other Western traditions is that it cannot be reduced to a set of doctrines or beliefs; instead, at its core is the conviction that we essentially need to keep listening to what our soul already knows, either in the particular circumstances of our lives or in matters more universal. We need this awareness among us again today, urgently.

This way of seeing and hearing has a particular lineage. It can be traced historically to the Celtic world, but this is not to say that it is bound to Celtic ethnicity and culture. It goes by other names in other places and times. It is not only for those who wear kilts and play bagpipes, for instance, or those who can claim to have an Irish granny. Nor is it bound religiously. Although the stream of wisdom that I will be drawing on here is largely from Celtic *Christian* teachers, it resonates with the deep spiritual wisdom of other great religious traditions as well.

The way of seeing that I am speaking about can be accessed by anyone, regardless of ethnic origin or religious background, for it is a way of seeing that is based on what the soul already deeply knows, that both the earth and every human being are sacred. And we can apply this way of seeing to the most pressing issues of humanity and the earth today.

In the Celtic tradition it was said that we suffer from soul-forgetfulness. We have forgotten who we are and have fallen out of true relationship with the earth and with one another. Thus, the path to well-being is not about becoming something other than ourselves or about acquiring a spiritual knowledge that is essentially foreign to us. It is about waking up to a knowledge that is deep in the very fabric of our being, and it is about living in relation to this wisdom.

Many years ago, shortly after I had written one of my earliest books, *Listening for the Heartbeat of God*, I was giving a talk on its main themes in a little church in Virginia. I was emphasizing the sacredness of the newborn child and the Light of the divine that is deep in every human being. I contrasted this belief with a teaching that has dominated so many other streams of Western Christian thought, the doctrine of original sin, in which it is taught that what is deepest in us or what is most original to our nature is opposed to God rather than being of God.

At the end of the talk a woman in her eighties came up the central aisle of the church with a copy of my book in hand. She was walking so purposefully that the naughty boy in me thought she was going to hit me over the head with it. But I was quite wrong. Instead, she said, "I want to show you what I wrote in this book after reading it." She then opened the front cover, and I saw that inside she had written, "I knew it! I knew it! I knew it!"

I often wish I had asked her for that copy of the book. She had expressed so succinctly what our experience is when we hear a truth that has been long neglected. We may never have heard it before. It may never have been taught to us. But when we do hear it, our response is, "Ah, I know this to be true, and some part of me has always known this."

Repeatedly, I hear similar exclamations from men and women in relation to the birth of their children or their earliest experiences of nature. Their words witness to our natural instinct for the sacredness of the birth of new life and of the earth itself. They are speaking of what at some level we all know. Their words have also increasingly led me to see that my primary role as a teacher of spirituality, and the role we can all play for one another in enabling spiritual awareness, is simply to try to utter what the soul already knows.

This knowing may have become buried under layers of cultural and religious conditioning and may need to be awakened. But the wisdom we are trying to give expression to is not just ours alone; it is also our listeners'. Our role is simply to set it free in one another, to bring it back up into consciousness. When we do release in each other a fuller awareness of the earth as sacred and of everything that has been born as holy, we will be changed by this awareness, and we will want to change the way the earth and its life-forms are being treated.

Sacred is the right word to convey this Celtic way of seeing, because it is a word that is not bound by religion. Inside the walls of religious practice, we speak of sacred scripture or sacred music, for instance, but way beyond those walls we also speak of the sacred universe or sacred moments. The word points with reverence to the divine essence of life and the true nature of relationship. When we speak of something as *sacred*, we are offering it ultimate respect. We are honoring it. We also invoke something of the power and authority of this word when we use the related term *sacrilege* to speak of the wrongs that are being done to the earth, to the creatures, and to other human beings. Etymologically, *sacrilege* means to try to take possession of the sacred, to use it for one's own ends rather than to reverence it.

In Celtic wisdom the sacred is as present on earth as it is in heaven, as immanent as it is transcendent, as human as it is divine, as physical as it is spiritual. The sacred can be breathed in, tasted, touched, heard, and seen as much in the body of the earth and the body of another living being as in the body of religion. It is the true essence of all life.

We speak of *Celtic* wisdom or a *Celtic* way of seeing, but who are the Celts? They are first referred to historically around 500 BCE. The Greeks called them *keltoi*, or "Celts." Around the same time the Romans referred to them as *galli*, or "Gaels." Today we primarily think of Ireland, Scotland, Wales, and Cornwall as Celtic territory, but in 500 BCE that was only the fringe. The Celts spanned the whole of middle Europe, ranging from what is now Turkey at the eastern edge right through to the Atlantic coastline of present-day Spain.

They were not an empire. Rather, the Celts formed a loose federation of tribes sharing a common culture and language base. They occupied Galatia (ancient Turkey), Galicia (ancient Spain), and Gaul (ancient France). All these place-names simply mean the "land of the Gaels" or "land of the Celts." They were primarily a rural and agricultural people; their architecture was inspired by nature, rounded and curved rather than square and rectangular. They had sophisticated trading networks and highly developed art forms, often reflecting nature's themes and patterns.

Roman historians speak of the Celts with perplexity when they describe them as worshipping without temples. This is because the Celts considered the forests and the mountains to be their temples. With even greater perplexity, Roman authors also describe them as viewing the feminine as sacred. In Rome, a thoroughly patriarchal society, this was considered unfathomable. But the Celts, who listened for truth deep within the human soul and the earth, prized the fact that all life comes from the union of the masculine and the feminine, which led them naturally and intuitively to honor the feminine as well as the masculine.

And so we get glimpses that take us to the edge of prehistory of a people who regarded the earth and the human mystery as sacred. We can access aspects of Celtic wisdom in pre-Christian form, but here I will be drawing primarily on the wisdom that has flowed to us over the centuries through *Christian* teachers in the Celtic world. Repeatedly, however, these teachers were to pose a challenge, and even a threat, to the way more prominent forms of Western Christianity viewed the sacred as separate from the ordinary rather than at the very heart of it.

The basis of this conflict was laid in the fourth century when Mediterranean Christianity became the religion of the empire. Empire did not want to be reminded that the earth and birth are sacred, a view that held too many implications for how living beings and the resources of the earth were to be reverenced rather than exploited. Consequently, religion was made to bow to imperial power, and the stage was set for conflict with the spirituality of the Celtic world. As we shall see, it is a conflict that has continued in various forms for over sixteen hundred years. The Celtic teachers who feature in this book help us remember that *all* life is holy, not just the life of *our* family or *our* race or *our* nation, and that *every* species, not just the *human* species, is sacred.

The focus of this book, however, is not simply looking back, and emphatically it does not pretend that we can *go* back, to a golden Celtic age. It is about accessing an ancient way of seeing in a fresh manner. In other words, the perennial wisdom of the Celtic world flows to us through teachers of the past, yet also invites us to be part of its further evolution and unfolding. Because it is a way of seeing that is based on paying attention to what is deepest in the human soul, rather than a fixed set of outward beliefs, it is a tradition that can evolve and grow with us on the journey. We are in need of a paradigm shift today, religiously, culturally, and ecologically, if the world as we know it is not to collapse. The Celtic tradition can assist us in reawakening to the sacred in ways that will inspire and sustain our journey forward.

My own realization that this lost tradition could be accessed again as part of a paradigm shift for today happened on the island of Iona, in the Inner Hebrides, off the western coast of Scotland. In my thirties, I had completed a doctorate in the Faculty of Theology at the University of Edinburgh and been ordained to the ministry of the Church of Scotland. My wife and I were appointed as coleaders of the abbey community on Iona, the sixth-century birthplace of Scottish Christianity and a place of international pilgrimage. In 563, St. Columba had led a Celtic mission from Ireland to this little island that sits out on the Atlantic edge of Great Britain.

Among my duties at the abbey was the responsibility for shaping morning and evening prayer. I began to make use of a collection of prayers and poetry that had come down over the centuries in oral tradition before being transcribed into written form in the nineteenth century. This poetry of soul had been spoken, chanted, or sung by men and women in the most ordinary contexts of daily life, at the rising of the sun and its setting, at the birth of a child and the death of a loved one, at recurring events in the endless cycle of the seasons. Here were prayers that deeply stirred my soul.

They wove together the physical and the spiritual, heaven and earth, the divine and the human in ways that allowed my soul to breathe deeply. They had further opened a window in me onto the sacredness of the natural.

Here I realized was treasure for today. It could serve our growing consciousness of the earth and the reintegration of the spiritual and the natural. So I wrote my first book, *Celtic Prayers from Iona*, in the hope that it might provide a "vocabulary of soul" for those of us seeking to integrate our spiritual practice with our love of the earth.

After Iona, when I was working at St Giles' Cathedral in Edinburgh in the mid-1990s, I began to realize that these beautiful prayers from the western islands of Scotland were not an exception in the Celtic world. They hadn't just appeared out of the blue. Rather, they were a particular expression of a way of seeing that could be traced from the earliest centuries right through to today. I woke up to what perhaps should have been perfectly obvious to me years earlier, that the nineteenth-century Scottish teacher I had done my doctoral research on in Edinburgh, Alexander John Scott, was in fact part of a stream of Celtic vision that had long preceded him and would continue to emerge again and again after him.

These were the realizations that prompted me eventually to write *Listening for the Heartbeat of God* (1997). It was a broad-brushstroke approach to the Celtic tradition that allowed many to access for the first time a Christian expression of looking for the sacred in all things. It was in this book that I developed one of the most cherished images of Celtic legend, the memory of John the Beloved, who, in leaning against Jesus at the Last Supper, was said to have heard the heartbeat of God. He became an image of the practice of listening for the beat of the sacred, deep in ourselves and one another and deep in the body of the earth. This was the image that then made its way right into the heart of my teachings and writings, in the hope that it would enable all of us to be more deeply aware of the sacred within every moment and every encounter. It was like a key for opening our consciousness to what the soul already knows, the sacredness of the earth and one another.

Simultaneously, I also came to realize more clearly that the consequences of not remembering the sacredness of the earth and the human soul are disastrous, both individually and collectively. This is what we are living in the midst of today, a planet struggling to breathe, religious fundamentalisms that are fueling hatred and violence, and refugee families throughout the world being denied sanctuary. These and so many more are evidence of a tragic breaking apart of our interrelationship, the failure of not remembering the sacred in one another.

Many years ago, I was giving a talk in Ottawa on some of these themes. I began the presentation by using a phrase from the prologue to St. John's Gospel, "The true light, which enlightens everyone, was coming into the world" (1:9). I spoke of the way the Celtic tradition invites us to look for this light in one another and in everything that has being. Attending the talk that evening was a young Mohawk elder who had been invited to be there specifically to make observations at the end of my talk about the resonances between Celtic and Native wisdom. The Mohawk elder stood with tears in his eyes as he spoke. He said, "As I have been listening to these themes, I have been wondering where I would be tonight, I have been wondering where my people would be tonight, and I have been wondering where we would be as a Western world tonight, if the mission that had come to us from Europe centuries ago had come expecting to find light in us."

Sometimes words cut us open with their power of truth. These words, spoken humbly by the Mohawk elder, pierced my heart with a truth that I have never forgotten. We cannot undo the tragic wrongs that have been done to Native American peoples during the westward expansion of settlement across what is now the United States and Canada, where indigenous human life was seen as having no value and viewed only as a hindrance in the quest for land and its resources. We cannot reverse the injustice, pain, and suffering that resulted from such horrendous greed and arrogance.

We can, however, be part of new beginnings. We can open ourselves to a radical humility of heart, which is our true strength, and look with expectation for the sacred deep within the "other"— the other individual, the other religion, the other race or nation or sexual orientation. And we can look with reverence to serve this sacredness in the other, to honor it, nurture it, and come into true relationship with it, allowing it to further reawaken in us the sacredness at the heart of our own being as well.

It has been such encounters and realizations over the years that have confirmed for me how imperative it is for us to share ways of seeing from our distinct spiritual traditions that can help reawaken us to the sacred in all things. This, I pray, is the longing that will be kindled in you throughout this book. It is time for us to remember, together.

As I have said, the purpose of this book is not to harken back to a past golden Celtic age. Instead, my goal is to equip readers with the teachings and practices of past Celtic leaders so that we can listen for the sacred and reverence it within us and all around us today. In the nine chapters of this book I invite you to access the wisdom of the Celtic world for today through the voices of nine historical figures. To show that the Celtic tradition is one that evolves and grows, I have chosen teachers from very different moments in history, representatives from the earliest Celtic Christian communities as well as those speaking to our times now.

The sacredness of the earth and the human soul is the broad canvas of this work, but each chapter explores a specific expression of the general theme, such as the sacredness of the feminine, the sacredness of the earth, or the sacredness of the imagination. Sometimes it comes in theological and philosophical form; at other times it is conveyed through myth and legend, poetry and imagination, or science and ecology. But whatever form it comes in, I offer it as a path of awareness to awaken us further to the sacred in all things.

These are the colors of the Celtic palette from which I paint the big picture. Each particular expression comes through the story of a historical teacher in the Celtic lineage of wisdom that spans nearly two thousand years. I treat each of these teachers as an icon for today to help reawaken us to the true heart of one another and the earth. At the end of each chapter, I provide a simple practice of meditative awareness for reflecting more deeply on the chapter's theme and exploring what it awakens in your life. These closing exercises are also collected in an appendix at the end of the book, which provides a nine-day cycle of meditative awareness that can be used on a daily basis to continue to access the wisdom of these iconic figures for today.

Chapter 1, "Sacred Soul," is about the first historically recorded writer in the British Celtic world, a monk named Pelagius. Around 400 CE he traveled from his homeland in Wales to Rome, where Christianity had become the religion of the empire and thus, at least in part, the servant of the empire. Pelagius challenged the theology at the heart of this alliance between power and religion. What is deepest in every human being, he taught, is sacred; we carry within us the dignity of the divine. This was a threat to the foundations of empire, which were built not on a reverence for, but domination of, people and the earth's resources. In the end, both empire and church denounced Pelagius, but this was not enough to silence him. His vision lived on, and it is rising among us again today, inspiring us to look for the sacred in every human being and to refuse to treat others merely as means to an end.

The second chapter, "Sacred Feminine," features Brigid of Kildare and the myths that surround this wise Irish woman of the fifth century. In Celtic legend she is a liminal figure, appearing at thresholds. She knows, for instance, the portals of birth and death. She meets us at the doorway between the divine and the human, humanity and the earth, the pre-Christian and the Christian. In all of these places she is a model of holding together apparent opposites. This is part of her feminine strength. She is faithful to the interrelationship of all things, including our relationship with the most vulnerable, those who seek shelter and refuge. Brigid shines in the Celtic imagination, reminding us to be true to one another and the earth and to never allow one expression of the sacred to dominate another—especially the way the masculine has dominated the feminine in much of Western history.

In Chapter 3, "Sacred Flow," we learn about the ninth-century Irish teacher John Scotus Eriugena and the figure of the *scotus vagans*, or "wandering Irish (monk)." Many of these wandering monks roamed mainland Europe to study and teach at this time.

They were scholars, not priests, and thus less bound by ecclesiastical control. In Eriugena's life and work we see Celtic wisdom taking on philosophical form. He develops not so much a theology of the sacred as a cosmology of the sacred. God is the sacred flow that runs through all things, the Light within all light, the Life that courses through the veins of the universe. At a time when ecclesiastically the Celtic way of seeing was regarded as heretical, Eriugena and other Irish scholars give it room to breathe in the realms of study and learning. They provide us today with a model of inner authority that can strengthen us in our prophetic stance against systems and outward authorities that are imperiling the very future of the earth.

Chapter 4, "Sacred Song," is about what happened to this way of seeing among ordinary people in places like the islands and Highlands of Scotland when the official religion of the land no longer tolerated expressions of Celtic wisdom. The sixteenth-century Reformation in Scotland, which separated the Scottish Church from Rome, did not in fact make any significant difference in the relationship between the church in power and ancient Celtic practices. That relationship simply found new form, and the Calvinism of the Scottish Reformation was even more hostile to Celtic teachings than the medieval Roman church had been, and it led eventually to persecution.

This gave rise to a spiritual resistance movement, especially among the Gaelic-speaking population of the country, for whom the ancient oral tradition of poetry and song was vital to preserving the memory of the sacred in all things. At the birth of a child or the death of a loved one, at the rising of the morning sun or the appearance of the moon at night, it was song and poetry that guarded and guided the threatened vision. As we shall see, an invaluable collection of song and prayer expressing this tradition was the *Carmina Gadelica*. Its words can help further awaken us to a spiritual vision of the intimacy of spirit and matter, nature and grace.

In the fifth chapter, "Sacred Imagination," we meet a young nineteenth-century Scottish minister, Alexander John Scott, who saw clearly again the sacred depths of the human soul. What is most truly human, he said, is what is most divine, and what is most truly divine is what is most human. A thread of the divine is woven through the fabric of the human soul and of everything that has being. This golden thread, he said, is our essence. For such teachings Scott was unanimously deposed from the ministry on a charge of heresy and banned from every pulpit in the land. Freed from the tight boundaries of religion, however, he began to access more deeply the human imagination as a powerful vehicle for reawakening the soul. Among the literature that he inspired were the novels and fairy tales of George MacDonald, which in turn influenced the imaginal works of C. S. Lewis and J. R. R. Tolkien. They provide us with models of the imaginative mind for today, so that we may be part of dreaming our way forward into a recovered sense of the sacred interrelationship of all things.

Chapter 6, "Sacred Earth," is about John Muir, perhaps the greatest modern prophet of ecological awareness and action. He saw nature's wildness as sacred and thus as in need of protection. His writings helped awaken the modern world to a new consciousness of the earth and the necessity of protecting earth's wildernesses. Prophetically, he denounced the widespread desecration of nature in nineteenth-century America and, equally prophetically, announced the sacredness of the earth in ways that invited his readers to get back in touch with the primal love of nature that stirs in our depths. In Muir we witness the Celtic way of seeing confronting the most significant issue facing humanity today, recognizing the sacredness of the earth and the need to come back into true relationship with her again.

Chapter 7, "Sacred Matter," concerns a twentieth-century resurrection of ancient Gallic vision by Pierre Teilhard de Chardin, a French scientist and priest. Teilhard saw that the deeper we move into the matter of the universe, the closer we come to the heart of the divine. At the heart of matter, he said, is the heart of God. This held radical implications not only for the church with regard to where the sacred is to be looked for and adored, but for the Western world at large in how we are to see and handle the matter of the earth. The Vatican forbade Teilhard from teaching and publishing. But before his death, in an act of priestly disobedience, he ensured that upon his death his writings would be released to the public. In these posthumous publications he prophetically called his readers to remember that the glory of the divine can be glimpsed deep in the translucence of earth's body, for all matter is sacred. He reminds us that religion is meant to serve and learn from the earth, not subjugate and exploit her. He models for us a path of courage in resisting powers that try to inhibit or diminish our sacred relationship with the earth.

Chapter 8, "Sacred Compassion," is about the urgency of transposing this vision of sacredness into practice. Matter matters, said George MacLeod, a prophet of Celtic awareness in twentieth-century Scotland. In particular this meant a just and compassionate handling of the earth's body as well as caring for the bodies of men and women everywhere. For MacLeod it meant the work of peacemaking among nations as well as contributing in one's own land to help shape a true vision of nationhood. In MacLeod we see a vital grounding of Celtic wisdom, translating what our soul deeply knows into compassion. He models for us a spirituality that embodies vision in action.

In Chapter 9, "Sacred Journey," we learn about how we can move forward. What are the new forms and expressions of reawakening to the sacred? The Scottish poet Kenneth White speaks of our need, first of all, to rediscover the earth and, in that deep rediscovery, to allow ourselves to reimagine the world, or what he calls a "rewording" of the world, seeing it and speaking it anew. This will prepare us for the journey toward what he calls a "new-found land," a way of being we have not yet experienced, inspired by the interrelationship of all things. We cannot yet know all the features of this new land, and indeed whether we will ever safely reach it, but we *can* know that our journey, both individually and together, must be guided above all else by a truthful relationship with the earth. To awaken to the sacred in all things is to embark on a pilgrimage into the unknown, a peregrination into a new landscape of soul. And, as we set sail, White teaches us about letting go of the old in order to open to the new.

Upon the publication of my last book, *The Rebirthing of God*, I was giving a talk in Dublin on the book's main themes. I spoke of the outward collapse of traditional Christianity in much of the Western world and asked what the new thing is that is trying to come forth from the heart of the Christian community at this moment in time. I also asked more generally what the yearnings for new birth stirring in the human soul today are, both individually and collectively—and not just religiously, but politically, economically, and culturally.

After my talk, an Irish sister spoke. For most of her religious vocation she had been a midwife, so she noted with interest the birthing imagery in the book. The God of so much of our Western Christianity, she said, is a pretty small God. We have created a deity that exists primarily to look after *our* religion, *our* nation, *our* species, *our* souls. But the new sense of the sacred that is trying to be born among us is like a cosmic God, much greater than any of the boundaries we have tried to set around sacredness. So, she concluded, we are in for quite a stretching!

I said to her, "Sister, why could I not have had this conversation with you before writing the epilogue to the book?" She had so simply and perfectly expressed what I had been trying to say. In a sense, this is exactly what the Celtic tradition has been saying all along, that we cannot contain the sacred. Rather, we are to look for it everywhere, and we are to serve it and be liberators of it in one another and in the earth.

I was so excited by the simplicity and power of the sister's image that when I phoned home to Edinburgh that night to speak about my day, I immediately shared the sister's image of the "great stretching." When my wife heard what the sister had said, she remembered an awareness that had come to her halfway through labor during our first child's birth, which was, "There's no going back!"

We can't go back. Knowing this is just as important as knowing that the labor pains of a new birthing will be mighty. There is no going back to the small God. We now know too much about the interrelatedness of all life to pretend that well-being can be sought for one part alone and not for the whole, for only one religion, one nation, one species. There is no returning to the limited notion of sacredness as if it were somehow the preserve of one particular people over another, of one race, gender, or sexual orientation. Sacredness is the birthright of all that is. It is the grace that comes with existence. It is not a feature of life that may or may not be there, depending on one's status, significance, or religious identification. It is the gift at the heart of every birth. It is life's essence, pure grace.

The Celtic way of seeing has a long lineage. Teacher after teacher in this tradition invites us to wake up to the earth and the human soul as sacred and to see this sacredness as beyond limitation, uncontained by any system or religion. It is a way of seeing that we can learn from now and bring to the most critical issues facing humanity today. It keeps opening and opening. And we can be part of its further unfolding for today as we yearn for the well-being that will come when we move back into faithful relationship with the true heart of one another and the earth as sacred.

SACRED SOUL: PELAGIUS

In Celtic wisdom we remember that our soul, the very heart of our being, is sacred. What is deepest in us is of God. Every child, every woman, every man, and every life-form is in essence divine. This is the truth that Pelagius invites us to remember.

Around 50 CE a shift began to occur in parts of the Celtic world, a transition from Druidic (pre-Christian) wisdom to Christian wisdom. St. Paul was teaching in Galatia around 55. Word of the mystery of Christ appears to have spread from the Celtic territory of Galatia into Gaul and Galicia and from there across the seas to Ireland and into ancient Britain. There was deep receptivity to the new teaching for, as we shall see, the Christ mystery did not seem strange to the Celtic worldview. Rather, it gave further expression to the sacredness the Celts already knew existed deep in the matter of the earth and in the stirrings of the human soul.

Significantly, news of the mystery of Christ traveled in spoken form. The Celts at this stage were not a literary people. Theirs was an oral culture. Wisdom was passed from generation to generation through poetry and storytelling. The message of Christ entered the Celtic world not in fixed written form, but in more fluid, spoken form. This made way for a rich intermingling of Christian and pre-Christian wisdom.

Historically, the earliest recorded Celtic Christian community was in Lyons in second-century Gaul. Roman writers refer to these Celts as irreligious and godless: irreligious, because they worshipped without temples in the wild, in forests and on mountains, which to the Celts were sacred; and godless, because they refused to worship the emperor, as part of the imperial cult of ancient Rome, which bestowed on the emperor divine authority. This in the end led to persecution and martyrdom among the Celts in Gaul.

The first Christian teacher of significance to emerge in Celtic territory was Irenaeus of Lyons (ca. 140–202). He had studied in Asia Minor (ancient Turkey) under Polycarp, who in turn had been a student of St. John in Ephesus, the disciple who was so cherished in Celtic legend. John had fled Jerusalem after the destruction of the Temple in 70 CE and made his home in that part of Asia Minor bordering the Celtic territory of Galatia.

Thus Irenaeus and John were only one teacher apart, and in Irenaeus we hear all the favorite themes of the Prologue to John's Gospel, for example, "In the beginning was the Word, and the Word was with God, and the Word was God" (1:1). As John goes on to say, everything has come into being through the Word.

Everything is essentially an utterance of the divine, a sacred sounding, each creature and life-form a unique and unrepeatable expression of the One.

Irenaeus had a Roman education, and so he was a literary figure, though he lived and taught in a predominantly oral culture. Three passionate concerns emerge in Irenaeus's writings.

First, he was opposed to the way in which celibacy, even as early as the second century, was beginning to be seen in Mediterranean Christianity as a higher path than marital union. He recognized celibacy as a distinct vocation, but refused to see it as a holier way. What nature shows us is that sexual relationship is an integral part of life's expression on earth. Sacredness for Irenaeus was not opposed to naturalness. A spiritual life therefore was not to be defined as contrary to sexual life and relationship. Thus, as early as the second century we find themes of holy naturalness emerging in Celtic wisdom.

Second, Irenaeus was concerned about a tendency to dilute the robust humanity of Jesus, a teaching that later came to be known as docetism. In the docetists' view Jesus only *seemed* to be human. He was divine, they said, and his humanity was merely an illusion, cloaking his divinity. Irenaeus, on the other hand, insisted that the divine and the human are to be held inseparably together. Jesus, as he put it, "ate butter and honey."[1] The divine and the human are one, he said. They are conjoined. Heaven is to be found in the things of earth. The divine is to be cherished within the earthliness of human life and relationship.

Irenaeus's third concern touches on the implications of reawakening to the body of the universe as sacred. He was concerned about a teaching that was gaining ground in second-century Christianity later known as *creatio ex nihilo*, "creation out of nothing." It taught that a distant Creator, purely transcendent, had fashioned matter out of nothing. Against this, Irenaeus taught that the universe is born out of the "substance" of God, not out of nothing.[2] In other words, the stuff of the body of the earth is sacred stuff. Therefore, how the body of another is handled in relationship, how the physical needs of those who are hungry and homeless are responded to, and how the body of the earth and its resources are treated—all these are holy matters.

As we shall see, this Celtic vision of earth's sacredness was to become a challenge to imperial power. When Christianity later became the religion of the empire in the fourth century, one of the first things expected of it, in return for political protection and prestige, was the doctrine of creation *ex nihilo*. Empire did not want to be told that matter is sacred, because then it could not do with impunity whatever it wished to matter. Then the body of the earth and the bodies of men and women were not just there to be used and exploited; they were to be honored and cared for.

The doctrine of creation *ex nihilo* formally declared that the earth consists of a substance that is neutral, not sacred. This gave the empire a type of permission to do whatever it wished with material things. It set the stage for how Christianity was to be used by empires again and again over the centuries—to sanction their exploitation of the earth.

If everything is essentially sacred, as Irenaeus taught, then what is the purpose of Christ? In so much of our Western theological inheritance, the Christ figure has been viewed as coming to save humanity from itself, to redeem it from its earthbound energies. Christ is represented as coming to airlift humanity into salvation. This led to a denial and sometimes even abuse of the physical rather than a reverencing of the earth and the human body.

This aspect of Western Christianity represents a betrayal of humanity's primal instinct for earth's sacredness, the knowing that fills our being, for instance, when we hold a newborn child in our arms and breathe in nature's holy purity in the scent of the child's skin; or the knowing that is beyond doubt in us when we taste heaven on the lips of another and know in our bodies the eternity of love; or the knowing that stirs in our depths when we witness the flowering and fruiting of the earth or watch the glory of a new day's light emerging from the darkness of night. This is a knowing that cannot be erased from the core of our being, and it is a knowing that spiritual vision and practice can help reawaken in us.

Irenaeus saw Christ not in opposition to this deep natural knowing, but as a radical affirmation of it. Christ, he said, is the "recapitulation" of the Word through which everything has come into being.[3] To recapitulate something is to say it again. It is to utter afresh what needs to be clarified or brought back into consciousness. So Irenaeus saw Christ not as a new Word, a Word that is somehow over against what is deepest in the earth and the human mystery. Rather, he saw Christ as respeaking the sacred essence of the universe, re-sounding the divine that is at the heart of all things. This was to see Christ as reawakening in humanity what it has forgotten.

Irenaeus's teaching carries significant implications for how we view the essence of our being. In Christian vocabulary it can be called our Christhood, the intersection of the divine and the human, the marriage of heaven and earth, that is deep within us. To awaken to this union is to experience recapitulation, or a re-sounding, of the deepest notes of our being. It is to find our true depths resounding with the vibration of the sacred in all things.

From Celtic Gaul and the teachings of someone like Irenaeus, the message of Christ spread to Celtic Britain and Ireland, likely by the end of the second century, still in oral form, and thus still with a fluidity that allowed a confluence with pre-Christian wisdom. It is not until the fourth century that we receive anything like a historical account of Celtic Christianity in Britain. By this stage in Rome, Mediterranean Christianity had become the imperial religion. But Celtic Britain was on the fringe of the empire, and the imperial army had never managed to occupy Ireland. Thus, the Celtic mission in Ireland and Britain was relatively free from the heavy hand of the empire.

The first writer and teacher of significance in Celtic Britain was a monk from Wales named Pelagius (ca. 360–430). He is perhaps the most misrepresented Christian teacher of all time, a misrepresentation that continues today. Most theological students in the Western world are required at some stage in their training to write an essay on the controversy between Pelagius and St. Augustine of Hippo (354–430), and it is assumed in advance who the hero will be and who the villain!

The misrepresentation is threefold. First, it is usually taught that there are no writings available from the hand of Pelagius, which means that all that can be learned about his teachings comes through the mouth of his theological opponent, Augustine. We now know that there are plenty of writings available from Pelagius, which gives us a fuller picture of what he actually taught.

The second misrepresentation is that there is usually no indication of where Pelagius came from or what his nationality was. Most theological students have graduated from seminary thinking that Pelagius was a one-off heretic who could have come from anywhere on earth. What we now know is that he was a Celt from Wales and that what he was teaching was not the idiosyncrasy of one particular teacher, but rather the vision at the heart of the Celtic mission.

The third and most widespread misrepresentation of all is the assumption that Pelagius believed we do not need grace, that humanity has the capacity to somehow save itself. What we now know from his writings is that he clearly taught the need for both grace and nature. But by grace he meant something very different from Augustine's conception of it. The latter believed that grace was given to save us from our nature, which was sinful. Pelagius, on the other hand, taught that grace was given to reconnect us to our nature, which was sacred and made of God. Divine grace is given not to make us something *other than* or *more than* natural. It is given to make us *truly* natural, to restore us to the sacred essence of our being.

Pelagius arrived in Rome early in the 380s. He became a teacher of note and a spiritual adviser to some of the leading families of the church in Rome. But almost immediately, controversy engulfed Pelagius. The church father Jerome and other teachers relentlessly criticized him, casting aspersions on his character as well as his teachings. Jerome, for instance, said that Pelagius was stupid from eating too much "Scottish porridge."[24]

Behind these attacks was a fear of what Pelagius was teaching, as a closer examination of the criticisms makes clear. First, he was accused by Jerome of spending too much time with women, teaching them how to read and interpret the scriptures. Jerome says that Pelagius was constantly among their spindles and wickerwork, as if that is all women might be doing. Already by the fourth century in Rome, the place of the feminine had been so subordinated within imperial Christianity that it was regarded as unacceptable for Pelagius to be teaching women to study and access scriptural learning (which is strange since the Gospels themselves show Jesus teaching women). The reality is that Pelagius was simply doing in Rome what the norm was in the Celtic Christian world—celebrating the sacredness of women and honoring their role in the study of wisdom.

Using a highly derisive word, Jerome described those who chose to study with Pelagius as "amazons."[5] The term means "without breasts," and in fourth-century Rome, long before the European discovery of South America, Jerome was implying that women who chose to read and study were denying their femininity.

The second principal criticism of Pelagius concerned his hairstyle. This may not seem a profound concern, but behind it lay one of imperial religion's biggest fears. The Roman clerical tonsure, a sign of priesthood, was characterized by a shaved crown surrounded by a ring of hair symbolizing the crown of thorns that had been placed on Jesus's head at his trial and crucifixion. Pelagius, on the other hand, wore what came to be known as the Celtic tonsure, which consisted of longer hair on top with the sides and back shaved more closely. Essentially, the Celtic tonsure had been the Druidic tonsure, one of the symbols of priesthood in pre-Christian Celtic custom. It spoke of the way in which the Celtic mission stood in radical continuity with the Druidic wisdom that had gone before it. To those in Rome, Pelagius had arrived looking like a pagan.

Devotion to Christ among the Celts did not mean abandoning the spiritual wisdom they had inherited from pre-Christian tradition, which celebrated the sacredness of the earth, the harmony of the spheres, and the wisdom of the human soul. Christ, they said, was their Druid (spiritual teacher), and the teachings and myths that had come down to them from their past were like an "Old Testament" that preceded Christ, not a contradiction to Christ. This conflicted with the belief system of the leaders of imperial Christianity, because for them anything pre-Christian was to be abandoned or eradicated but certainly not honored.

The third and primary criticism of Pelagius focused on his belief that when we look into the face of a newborn, we are looking into the face of God freshly born among us. Pelagius was not speaking merely of the newborn child. He was speaking also of what is deepest in every human being. He was enunciating the "dignity" of our human nature, as he put it, not the defilement of our nature.[6] He was emphasizing our sacredness over our sinfulness. This, as we shall see, did not mean that Pelagius was naive about humanity's capacity for falseness. Rather, he was teaching that what is deepest in us is *of* God, not *opposed* to God. It is this, he said, that we can clearly see in the face of a newborn child.

We know this to be true of the newborn child, do we not? We know that, although our children have come through us, they issue from a source deeper than us. In their face we glimpse something of the Light from which all life has come. In their skin we smell the freshness of life's origins. It is this deep natural knowing that Celtic wisdom builds on. It is a sacred knowing that becomes the basis of spiritual vision.

As early as 413 in northern Africa, Augustine was preaching against Pelagius, who by now was in Palestine, having fled to the Middle East as a refugee after the sack of Rome in 410. Augustine was preparing the ground for imperial Christianity's doctrine of original sin, the belief that at birth we are essentially bereft of God rather than born of God—corrupted, not sacred. Once again, the religion of the empire was about to formalize a teaching that was convenient for imperial power, enabling empire to relativize people's worth rather than reverence their dignity.

In 415 Augustine sent his disciple Orosius to Palestine to have Pelagius tried for heresy. Two Palestinian church synods, which were like diocesan councils under the leadership of a bishop, examined Pelagius's teachings, and both found him innocent. But these decisions were a reflection of Eastern Christian belief, which never accepted the doctrine of original sin. What later came to be known as Eastern Orthodoxy, including the Greek, Russian, and Syrian Orthodox communions, celebrates human nature as sacred, essentially blessed at birth rather than essentially sinful.

Augustine and the African bishops convened two synods of their own in 416, which found Pelagius guilty of heresy. Emboldened, in 417 the African leadership petitioned Zosimus, the bishop of Rome, to have Pelagius excommunicated. He examined Pelagius's teachings and found him innocent of heresy. Zosimus, however, is a Greek name, suggesting that Zosimus had likely been influenced by Eastern Christian perspectives. He proceeded to write to Augustine and the African bishops, saying, "Love peace, prize love, strive after harmony."[7] The tragedy is that Augustine ignored the advice.

Denied the support of the bishop of Rome, Augustine now went directly to the emperor, and in the spring of 418 Pelagius was banned from the empire on a charge of disturbing the peace. A few months later, imperial religion did what it was created to do, serve the empire. In the meantime, Zosimus had died and another pope was in place, so Pelagius was excommunicated.

The imperial ban against Pelagius on a charge of disturbing the peace was likely related to his teachings on the sacredness of nature as well as the essential sacredness of humanity. He had been insisting that just as grace is of God, so nature is of God. Just as the elements of the sacrament of grace, namely, the bread and wine of the Eucharist, are to be justly shared, so the elements of the sacrament of nature, the altar of the earth and its resources, are to be equitably shared.

Pelagius taught that there are three types of people: those with enough, those with more than enough, and those with not enough, and the primary reason some do not have enough is because others have more than enough. "A person who is rich," he said, "and yet refuses to give food to the hungry may cause far more deaths than even the cruelest murderer."[8]

After his ban and excommunication from the church, Pelagius fled to the relative safety of his homeland, Wales, as well as residing for some time in Ireland, territory that was entirely free from Roman control. From there he continued to write. To ensure that his writings would circulate freely throughout the empire, he wrote under pseudonyms, most frequently under the name Augustine. An expression of Celtic humor!

In Pelagius's teachings we can identify a fivefold focus: the sacredness of the human soul, the sacredness of nature, the sacredness of spiritual practice, the sacredness of wisdom, and the sacredness of compassion.

First, Pelagius, as we've seen, taught the sacredness of the human soul. The essence of our nature is of God. But this inner nobility can become "buried," he says, covered over by falseness and delusion.[9] We become addicts to what is false and, in a drunken spiral, slip further and further into insensitivity and wrong. He believed the sacred essence of our being is never undone. Always it is there in our depths to rise again with the assistance of what he calls "divine grace."[10]

Pelagius had been accused by Augustine of teaching that we have the capacity to save ourselves and that therefore we do not need grace, but Pelagius not only insists on the imperative of grace; we find him emphasizing three types of grace.[11] The first is what can be called the grace of nature, or original grace, by which he means that all is grace. The gift of this moment, the gift of the rising sun and of all that grows from the ground, the gift of our birth and our children's births, the gift of thought and dreaming and waking and loving—all sheer grace.

Also there is the grace of illumination, when we experience a cleansing of our inner sight and we see clearly again. We awaken to a way of seeing that we have forgotten. We see again the sacred shining deep in all things. This is the grace that invites us back into true relationship with the heart of everything that has being. And, finally, there is the grace of forgiveness or mercy. When we have failed, when we have betrayed another, when we have done what is wrong, the grace of forgiveness is given that we may live again from our true depths.

The second main theme that we can discern in Pelagius's teachings is the sacredness of nature. "Narrow shafts of divine light," he says, "pierce the veil that separates heaven from earth."[12] These shafts of divine Light can be glimpsed everywhere, in every creature, every life-form, every human being. They come not from without but from deep within, from the Light that is within all life. God's spirit is in all living things, he says, "and if we look with God's eyes, nothing on the earth is ugly."[13] This belief held radical implications for Pelagius. It led him to call on the fourth-century Roman Empire to treat the body of the earth and its resources with reverence and see that it was equitably shared.

The sacredness of spiritual practice is the third main theme that can be identified in Pelagius's teachings. Meditative prayer, he said, is like plowing the "fertile soil" of our soul.[14] It is like till-ing the inner fields of our being to uncover truth. For Pelagius, this inner work of awareness necessitates having a soul friend, or *anamchara*, as he called it. Pelagius is the first teacher in the Celtic world to explicitly refer to this spiritual practice. A person without a soul friend is like a body without a head, he said. In other words, it is vital for us in our personal journey of inner awakening to have a friend who knows the depths of the soul, to whom we can unin-hibitedly show what is stirring within us.

"We must open our souls completely to this friend," said Pe-lagius, "hiding nothing and revealing everything."[15] This is not because our soul friend knows more about what is stirring in us than we do. It is because the very act of trying to give expression to our soul, in the presence of someone who loves and trusts us, will enable us to grow in awareness. Then what may have been lying unconscious in our depths will move up into greater con-sciousness, further enabling us to translate this awareness into action in our lives and relationships in the world.

A lovely story tells of a young woman named Celantia, who asked Pelagius for a rule of life. "Tell me how to live," she begged. To which Pelagius responded, "Don't ask me." The source of such a rule "is inside your own heart," he said.[16] She needed to learn to read in her own heart the truth of what God has written. When she had learned to read the inner text of her being, she was to write it out in her own hand and allow that to be her rule of life.

But then Pelagius added an important warning: if what she read within herself was in conflict with the teachings of Jesus, then she had misread her heart, and she must go back and read again.

This story is important for at least two reasons. First, it is saying that we all need to do our own inner reading. No one else can do this for us. Yes, we need to read our soul in relationship and in conversation with our *anamchara* and others in community, but each one of us needs to take responsibility for the holy work of inner attentiveness. Truth is not simply to be dispensed from above. It is to be mined from within. Second, Pelagius's response to Celantia is saying that the teachings of Jesus are like a touchstone for the soul, a measuring rod of inner wisdom. Jesus does not embody a truth that is foreign to us. Rather, he discloses to us the essence of our soul, from which we have become distant. It is about waking up to what is already there.

The fourth theme of sacredness in Pelagius is that of wisdom. He sees this as the birthright or property of the human soul. Drawing heavily from the wisdom literature of the Hebrew scriptures, he speaks of wisdom being fashioned within us in our mother's womb. It is innate to the sacredness of our being, pure gift, planted deep within, although it is our responsibility to help bring it up into consciousness. This leads Pelagius to look for wisdom, and to expect to find it, way beyond the bounds of Christianity, in every culture, every religion, and every people.

He appeals to the literary figure Job in the Hebrew scriptures, who can be viewed as a prototype of human wisdom long before the birth of Christianity. "What a man Job was," he says, "a man of the gospel before the gospel was known." He opened up the hidden wealth of wisdom in our nature and brought it out into the open. Job, he continues, "has taught us how great is that treasure in the soul which we possess but fail to use and, because we refuse to display it, believe that we do not possess it either."[17] Sacred wisdom is deep in our nature. The journey to wholeness is about awakening to this wisdom deep within and seeking it everywhere, in every culture and every religion.

The fifth theme that appears in Pelagius's teachings is the sacredness of compassion. Pelagius taught that it is not so much what you believe *about* Jesus that matters. The important thing is becoming *like* Jesus, becoming compassionate. A Christ-one, he said, is one "who shows compassion to all, . . . who feels another's pain as if it were his own, and who is moved to tears by the tears of others."[18] And this compassion is not just for human beings, he said; it is for all life. "When Jesus commands us to love our neighbors, he does not only mean our human neighbors; he means all the animals and birds, insects and plants, amongst whom we live."[19]

It is the sacredness of compassion that fuels the holy work of justice. It is compassion within us and among us that will inspire and sustain the work of equitably accessing the earth's resources. Pelagius asks, are the glowing lights of the moon or the stars given to "serve the rich man more than the poor"?[20] Of course not; they are for all. So it is, he insists, with the Light that is within all things. The great resources of land and sea, these too are for all. They are given for the well-being of every people and every nation, not just for the well-being of some.

All of these themes of sacredness clashed with the way empire worked. They were like seeds of radicalism. The sacredness of the human soul: people are not just there to be controlled and used, but should be reverenced and related to. The sacredness of nature: we cannot do whatever we wish to the body of the earth, but are to honor it as our own body. The sacredness of spiritual practice: truth is not just dispensed from above by those who are in power, but accessed from deep within by everyone. The sacredness of wisdom: one nation, or culture, or religion does not have a monopoly on wisdom; it is to be found in all people, all cultures, all religions. The sacredness of compassion: we are to see and feel and act for others as we see and feel and act for ourselves. All of this challenged the inequities upon which the empire was built.

Although Pelagius was banned in the year 418, the ban was not enough. Three years later, in 421, another imperial edict banned all those who followed the teachings of Pelagius from coming within one hundred miles of Rome. Still threatened, the empire took additional steps. In 428, ten years after the initial judgment, another edict prevented followers of Pelagius from being anywhere in Italy. And if this still was not enough, over one hundred years later, in 529, Pelagius's teachings were condemned by another church council. How many times does one man need to be condemned by the empire and its church?

And finally, over two hundred years after Pelagius's ban and excommunication, the bishop of Rome complained in a papal encyclical of 640 that the "pernicious" teachings of Pelagius were still rampant in Ireland. He demanded that the Irish "expel the venom of this wicked superstition" from among them.[21] The ban did not work. Bans never work against what the soul knows. Truth will always rise again.

Pelagius wrote to another young woman who was seeking his counsel:

> *Have regard for your origin, consider your lineage, respect the honor of your noble stock. Acknowledge you are not only the daughter of a man [and a woman], but the daughter of God as well, graced with the nobility of divine birth. Present yourself in such a way that . . . your divine nobility shines forth clearly.*[22]

We have been graced with the nobility of divine birth. The essence of our being is sacred. Shall we be true to it in one another? Shall we be true to it in ourselves?

Pelagius is an icon for us today of reawakening to the sacredness of every human being. He was faithful to this vision even at great cost to himself. The mightiest empire on earth banished him, and the imperial church excommunicated him, but this was not enough to quench the vision that he expressed in his life and teachings. It lived on. And it still lives on.

We are living at a critical moment of history. Will we truly awaken to the sacredness of every person regardless of gender, race, or religion? Holders of power, both political and religious, are obstructing this work, and some of them are even denying the need for it. But they cannot destroy the vision of sacredness that has welled up again and again over the centuries and is now demanding our attention, perhaps like never before. There is hope. And it is a hope based on our deepest knowing, that every human being is sacred, body and soul.

Before concluding this chapter, I invite you to take a few minutes to pay attention to what Pelagius has awakened in you. As you do the reflection practice below, sitting in silence, name in gratitude what has been stirring within you from this chapter. (All of the meditative practices are collected in the appendix, which can be used on a daily basis to remain alert to what has been calling your inner attention as you read this book.)

Reflection: Sacred Soul

Words of Awareness

You have been graced with the dignity of divine birth, says Pelagius. Live this dignity in your life, safeguard it in one another, and protect it in every human being.

(Reflect for a brief time on the ways this wisdom applies to your life.)

Prayer of Awareness

Awake, O my soul,
And know the sacred dignity of your being.
Awake to it in every living soul this day.
Honor it, defend it,
In heart and mind, in word and deed.
Awake, O my soul,
And know the sacred dignity of your being.

(Listen silently for a few minutes within the sacredness of your being.)

Awake, O my soul. Awake.

SACRED FEMININE:
ST. BRIGID OF KILDARE

Celtic wisdom remembers the sacredness of the feminine. Deep within us and deep within the matter of the universe is a conjoining of masculine and feminine energy. Both are of God. Both are essential to us, individually and as a species. At the heart of the marriage of heaven and earth is a dance. When the sacred feminine and masculine move as one within us and make love, we are well. It is to this that the stories and legends of Brigid of Kildare invite us to awaken.

Probably the most beloved of Celtic saints is the golden-haired Brigid of Kildare (ca. 451–523). She is the saint who loves the earth, who reveals the sacredness of the feminine, who models female leadership, inspires poets and musicians, midwifes at new beginnings, and extravagantly embodies compassion and boundless generosity toward the poor and those who seek refuge. We need her among us again today.

We know little about Brigid historically. The first biographies of her, more hagiographical than historical, were written over a hundred years after her death. Brigid's life is shrouded in myth and legend. So, in a sense, the question before us is not so much who she *was*, but rather who she has *become* in the Celtic heart and imagination over the centuries.

Legend has it that Brigid was born just before sunrise, in the twilight of early morning, in that time governed neither by the sun's light nor the moon's light, but by the two lights, the twi-light. It is also said that her mother gave birth to her neither within the house nor outside, but at the threshold of the dwelling. So her birth signals that she will be associated with the meeting place between opposites, the night and the day, the sun and the moon, the within and the without. She occupies the liminal space between worlds. She stands at the doorway or meeting place between the so-called opposite dimensions of life, which have been torn apart from each other.

In this chapter we will explore four thresholds, or liminalities, through the lens of Brigid: the doorway between the pre-Christian and the Christian, the portal between the divine and the human, the relationship between humanity and the earth, and the liminal space between the womb of the universe and what is trying to come into being.

The first threshold, then, is the doorway between the pre-Christian and the Christian. Brigid awakens us to be receptive to sacred wisdom well beyond the bounds of our own spiritual tradition and culture.

According to legend, Brigid was the midwife at the birth of the Christ Child. It poses no problem for the Celtic imagination that a fifth-century Irish saint should be present at the birth of the Christ Child in first-century Palestine! Imagination makes two worlds one, or, more specifically, it speaks from the one world within all worlds, the eternal dimension deep in every place and time and at the heart of every people and tradition.

The Hebridean version of the legend is that Brigid was the barmaid at the inn in Bethlehem.¹ The inn was full. It was a time of scarcity and famine in the land. Brigid had been given instructions by the innkeeper not to welcome anyone else into the inn and also not to share food or drink with passersby. She herself had only a cup of water left and a bannock, an unleavened oatmeal or barley loaf.

Strangers come to the door of the inn—an older man with gray in his beard and a woman who is young and beautiful. Her lips are red and her cheeks ruddy with youth. She has long golden hair and blue eyes, and her belly is rounded like autumn fruit ready to drop. Brigid is not able to welcome them into the inn because it is full, but she shares with them at the door her remaining cup of water and loaf of bread.

The strangers then move on. But when Brigid returns to the kitchen, she finds that her cup of water has been replenished and her loaf of bread restored. Pondering what this might mean, she looks out of the window and sees a great light shining from the byre, the cow barn. Rushing out, she enters the byre to find the young woman, Mary, in labor. Brigid kneels before her and mid-wifes at the birth of the child. She holds him high in her arms to give thanks for the birth and then suckles him at her breast.

Thus, Brigid came to be known as both the midwife and the wet nurse of the Christ Child. The legend points to the way in which she midwifed the birth of Christianity in Ireland and how she nurtured it with her own being. But for Brigid the birthing of a devotion to Christ in Ireland did not mean the abandonment of pre-Christian wisdom.

It is said that Brigid's mother was a Christian and her father, or stepfather, a Druid, a spiritual leader in pre-Christian Celtic society vested with religious, judicial, and political authority. One strand of legend even says that she grew up on Iona among the Druids. The isle of Iona, typically among sacred sites in the Celtic Christian world, had been a Druidic place of pilgrimage long before it became associated with St. Columba in the sixth century. We do not know exactly what Brigid's relationship with Iona and the western islands of Scotland was. We do know, however, that these islands are called the Hebrides, meaning the "islands of Brigid, or Bride," as she is often called in Scotland. We know that she was held in the deepest of affection in Hebridean legend and lore. She is a symbol of continuity in the Celtic world between one age of wisdom and the next.

A painting in the National Galleries of Scotland in Edinburgh called "St Bride," by the Scottish artist John Duncan (1866–1945), depicts Brigid being carried by the angels from Iona to Palestine for the birth of the Christ Child. Her golden hair is flowing in the wind over the waters of the Sound of Iona. The two angels carrying her are magnificently attired in garments displaying scenes from scripture, including that of John the Beloved leaning against Jesus at the Last Supper. Seals are leaping from the water and birds are winging their way through the air beside her, longing to be with Brigid for the sacred birth of the Child, born of heaven, born of earth. In the background of the painting is an island with a church tower in silhouette against the colored sky. It is the Benedictine abbey on Iona—from the thirteenth century! Different times are woven together as one, and the pre-Christian merges into the Christian. The sacred story flows like a subterranean stream from one era into the next.

The Book of Leinster, a twelfth-century Irish manuscript, says that Brigid was a Druidess. It seems that she was not only a member of the Druidic community of the Holy Oak in Leinster, but its leader, and that this community was the most significant Druidic site in Ireland. Oaks were especially sacred to the Druids. They established their communities by great oak trees and in oak groves. The word *druid* simply means "oak-knower" or "bearer of oak wisdom." It was a way of knowing that, like the ancient oaks, which reached deep into the ground with their roots and high into the air with their mighty branches, connected heaven and earth. Brigid's community was located by one of the great ancient oaks of Ireland, possibly over a thousand years old.

When Brigid, to use St. Columba's later expression, came to see Christ as her Druid, she brought with her an entire Druidic community as well as much of Ireland. She became Mary of the Gaels, the Mother of Christ to the Irish people, and her community became known as Kildare, which means "Church of the Oaks." The great Druidic site of Leinster had made its transition into embracing the Christ mystery, but without abandoning the spiritual wisdom that had preceded Christianity.

The pre-Christian focus of Brigid's community had been devotion to the earth goddess and the mystery of new life forever rising from deep within. The name of the pre-Christian earth goddess was Brigid, which means "great one" or "shining one." So it is likely that Brigid was not the saint's birth name, but rather the name bestowed upon her as leader of the Druidic community. She represented the goddess and thus came to bear her name.

Like so many Gaelic words, the name Brigid is related to Sanskrit, in this case the Sanskrit word *brihati*, which means "brightness." The earth goddess was the shining or brightness deep in all things. She was described in terms of immanence rather than transcendence. There were no carved anthropomorphic images of the goddess Brigid. She was sought and reverenced in the rivers and streams, in the forests and mountains rather than in the heavens.

The St. Brigid myths weave together the pre-Christian and Christian. She combines the Druidic love of earth with Christianity's awareness of heaven. She points to a sacredness that is within as well as beyond us, that is embodied in earth but not bound by form, a sacredness that is beneath our very feet yet higher than the highest heaven, the two forever one, both expressing the divine essence of life.

During St. Brigid's lifetime, but especially in the centuries after her death, it can be said that the goddess Brigid transitioned or shape-shifted into the saint Brigid. In Celtic imagination, the saint took on many of the characteristics of the goddess. This meant that certain pre-Christian rituals connected with her continued naturally in Kildare and were cherished for hundreds of years, especially the ritual of the perpetual fire.

For centuries, a fire had been kept burning continuously in the Druidic community of Leinster to celebrate the Light shining deep in all things, the light that has not been overcome by the darkness. In Kildare, this continued for over a thousand years into the Christian era. The flame was kept burning, day after day, night after night, tended to by the sisters of the community of Brigid, who faithfully took turns keeping it alive. Not until the sixteenth century was it extinguished, violently, at the hands of Protestant Reformers. This marked a tragic shift in Ireland's dominant form of Christianity away from the divine as immanent and feminine toward regarding it solely as masculine and transcendent. The marriage of so-called opposites had been torn apart, and the celebration of the sacred feminine now became suspect.

But even after the fire was extinguished in Kildare, a parallel spiritual practice continued among the people. Just as in first-century Palestine after the destruction of the Temple, a persecuted Judaism developed family table–based rituals of Sabbath observance and prayer to keep alive its inherited wisdom, so in the Celtic world at this time there emerged the practice of keeping a perpetual fire in the family hearth. In the Hebrides it was called tending the mother fire and was associated especially with the feminine and the Light of the divine that is deep in matter.

There were homes in the Hebrides of Scotland in which the mother fire was kept burning continuously for hundreds of years. The ritual of the hearth was presided over by the eldest woman of the household. At the end of the day, as the family prepared for rest, she would rake the glowing embers in the fireplace into a circle and place three pieces of peat on the fire. Then she would cover it, which was called the *smooring* of the fire, with enough ashes to subdue the fire without extinguishing it. At the same time, she would invoke the blessing of Brigid on the household and its land and creatures.[2] Then in the morning she would raise the mother fire back up into full flame, symbolizing the light that will not be overcome by darkness.

This was only one of many pre-Christian rituals that continued in the Celtic Christian world. It is even likely that the Irish cross, sometimes called St. Brigid's cross, carries within it features of pre-Christian symbolism. The Irish cross form is a symbol that we find in many ancient cultures, including those in India. With its four equal arms, depicted almost in rotating motion, it can represent the sun emerging from the winter darkness of the earth, rotating through the four seasons of spring, summer, autumn, and winter before being reborn into a fresh coming of light in the spring.

A story is told of Brigid sitting at the deathbed of a pagan Irish prince. Wanting to share with him the mystery of Christ, she picked up some straw from the floor and wove it into a four-armed reed cross, of which he would have known the pre-Christian significance. She then said to the prince that, just as the sun's light is not overcome by the darkness of winter, so Christ reveals that the sacred Light within us will not be overcome by the dark, even the darkness of death. The prince then received from Brigid anointing with oil, a symbol of Christ and healing, and died in peace. Brigid combines within herself the ancient ways of Ireland with a devotion to the wisdom of Christ.

Another pre-Christian element that continued in Kildare was the mixed nature of monastic life, men and women living together in community under the leadership of a woman. This was a mark of the honoring of the feminine in pre-Christian Ireland that Brigid transposed into Christian form. We know, for instance, that women were celebrating the Mass in Ireland until at least the sixth century. In 520 a synod of bishops in Rome denounced the practice as "abominable" and called on the Irish to forsake their sinful ways![3]

As abbess of Kildare, Brigid had episcopal status in the Celtic world. A later account, not knowing what to make of a woman in this role, said that her consecration as bishop had been "accidental." Bishop Mel, who was consecrating her, had read from the wrong service book, it claimed. The bishop had been so "intoxicated with the grace of God" that he had not known what he was doing![4] Brigid and her community carry into the Christian era a deep reverencing of the feminine.

She is a model for us of standing in the doorway between the wisdom of our spiritual tradition and the wisdom of traditions that have gone before or alongside us. At the doorway between faiths we can stand and bow, awakening to what the soul deeply knows, that wisdom is to be found and reverenced way beyond the boundaries of any one tradition. We need these many wisdom traditions. They are given not to compete with each other, but to complete each other.

The second liminality to be explored through Brigid is the way she appears in the portal between the divine and the human. She has been seen by Celts over the centuries as bearing the energies of the sacred in ways that express the intermingling of the divine and the human that is in all people.

Brigid, as we have already noted, was honored in Ireland as Mary of the Gaels. In the Hebrides she was called the "foster mother of Christ," and the Christ Child was spoken of as the "little fosterling of Bride."[5] Fostering was a cherished role in the Celtic world. Often Celtic princes and princesses would have their children fostered by extended members of the family as a way of ensuring peace across the tribe. In Celtic imagination Brigid fosters what is born of the marriage of heaven and earth within us and within all things. To put it in Christian terms, it is the Christhood of our being that she nurtures, the intermingling of the divine and the human within us.

She has been so loved among the Celts that at times she outshines Mary. In a sense she takes on Mary's role, and her name is invoked in many prayers, including the beautiful tradition of sleep consecration in which the divine is invited into the sacred realm of sleep and dream life:

I lie down this night with God,
and God will lie down with me.
I lie down this night with Christ,
and Christ will lie down with me.
I lie down this night with the Spirit,
and the Spirit will lie down with me.
God and Christ and the Spirit
be lying down with me.[6]

Some of these sleep consecrations also include Brigid:

I lie down tonight . . .
with Bride beneath her mantle.[7]

Lying down with Brigid under her cloak represents the intimacy of
the divine and the human; they meet under her mantle, wrapped
as one. The sacred is known in this intimacy.

In parts of Ireland today, in Galway, for example, one can still
hear people, particularly older men and women, using Brigid's
name in greetings and farewells. "May God, Mary, and Brigid be
with you," they say. The Irish often use sacred names in everyday
speech, sometimes as exclamations, at other times simply for added
emphasis. "God, Christ, Almighty, you are beautiful," they might
say to you. Or, if the weather has been bad, you may hear, "Jesus,
Mary, and Joseph, it's been a rainy day."

This is all part of holding heaven and earth together, invoking
sacred names in everyday conversation to remember the interweaving of the divine and the human that is within us all. The name of
Brigid is particularly used to speak of the immediacy of the sacred.
She stands at the doorway of every encounter, inviting us to look
for the sacred in everyone, including the stranger, the foreigner,
and the other, and in the depths of our own being too.

In the Hebrides there is an ancient rune of hospitality attributed to Brigid, in which the welcoming of the stranger is

viewed as a welcoming of Christ.[8] Brigid inspires an expectation of finding the sacred beyond the bounds of one's religion, culture, or nation. It is about being open to the heart of the other, ready to receive blessing from those on the other side of accentuated lines of division. It is about awakening to the holy in the other.

Stories of Brigid's generosity abound. As a girl she was known for giving away her family's milk, butter, and cheese to passersby. As abbess of Kildare she was remembered for sometimes parting with the most cherished liturgical garments of her religious community to feed the poor. Perhaps most famously of all, as a young woman she gave away her father's bejeweled sword to a beggar. Her father went to the king of Leinster to complain about her. "She does things without asking permission," he said.[9]

This is part of why we need Brigid among us today. There are certain things we need to do without waiting for permission, for example, giving sanctuary in our nation to refugee families who need shelter and protection from harm. This is a divine imperative, and it is dependent not upon getting outward permission but upon getting in touch with the most sacred imperatives of the soul. Brigid reminds us how to stand by what we know to be true, positioning ourselves with courage at the doorway of compassion.

Cogitosus, the seventh-century biographer of Brigid, says that no one was ever refused food, clothing, or sanctuary in Kildare. Interestingly, he calls it the "monastic city" of Kildare.[10] This term clarifies for us the nature of monastic life in the Celtic world.

These were not secluded, cloistered monks and nuns living a life set apart from the rest of the population. Rather, they were men and women living their monastic vocation together in the midst of and in connection with larger settlements. In Kildare, the monastic community was the core of the "city," and in orbit around the monastery were networks of farmers and traders, artists and musicians. Celtic monastic life was at the heart of an unfolding Irish civilization, and what Cogitosus enables us to see in the case of Kildare is that this city was a sanctuary city.

Brigid shows us a way of living from our true depths of compassion, inspiring us to create sanctuary for those in need, to be sanctuary communities, churches, nations. She invites us to look for the sacred in the stranger, in the other, in the foreigner, to look with faith rather than primarily with fear.

Brigid's most extravagant generosity was the way she shared beer with the poor, especially during Eastertide, the season in which new life and new beginnings are celebrated. Legend has it that, if there was no beer to be found, Brigid would turn water into beer, so that the poor could freely celebrate. "Better beer than has ever been brewed in all the world," adds one account![11] Or as an eighth-century manuscript known as Brigid's *Quiver of Divine Desires* puts it:

> *I should like a great lake of ale*
> *for the King of kings.*
> *I should like the angels of Heaven*

to be drinking it through time eternal....

I should like cheerfulness to be in their drinking.

I should like Jesus to be there among them.

I should like the three Mary's of illustrious renown to be
  with us.

I should like the people of heaven, the poor, to be
gathered around us from all parts.[12]

Is it any wonder that Brigid outshines Mary in the affection of the Gaels? She extravagantly embodies the sacred generosity that is born from the marriage of the human and the divine within us.

St. Brigid's feast day is February 1. The evening of January 31, the day before St. Brigid's Day, was one of the greatest celebrations in the Celtic year, on a par with Christmas Eve. The rituals celebrated that evening were called Threshold Rites, which included literally standing at the doorway of one's house invoking Brigid's presence and keeping a place for her that evening at the family table and beside the family hearth. Symbolically, Brigid's Eve was at the threshold between light and dark, between the winter solstice and the spring equinox. It was also viewed as a threshold between heaven and earth, and Brigid and those who had gone ahead through the veil of death were thought to be especially close that night.

Similarly, it was a threshold between the masculine and the

feminine, as the women of the community presided at the feast and the men were required to beg—playfully, but nevertheless to beg—to attend the celebration. As a threshold also between the rich and the poor, the best food and drink was kept for the poorest in the community, especially the most elderly women. It was even a threshold between humanity and the creatures, as special treats were given that night to the cattle and horses.

Brigid invites us to be aware of thresholds that we are in the midst of, both individually and together, at the changing of seasons, at the dawning of the day, and in the approach of nightfall. Similarly, threshold times in our lives include transitions in work, resettling as families, the births of our children, new seasons in our lives, endings and partings, and times of letting go. It can be important to create simple threshold rites and practices for these transition moments, for instance, the lighting of candles, standing together at an archway, walking a labyrinth, or undertaking a pilgrimage route. These can help us remain alert to the meeting of the divine and the human at the heart of our being. The portal is always near. We need simply open to it.

The intimate relationship between humanity and the earth is the third liminality that we find in connection with Brigid. Brigid is close to the earth, of the earth. Her feast day, as we have noted, is February 1, which in the Celtic world is the first day of spring.

The symbolism of spring energy thus abounds in Brigid myths. In pre-Christian Celtic observance, February 1 was also the feast day of the earth goddess, a celebration known in the Celtic calendar as *imbolc*, which means "in the belly." This is where new life is to be found, in the belly of the earth, in the belly of the feminine, in the belly of the human soul. Brigid is associated with the stirrings of new life from these depths.

In pre-Christian legend it was said that on February 1 the Hag of Winter, Cailleach, would journey to what was called the "mystical island" in the sea to drink from its Well of Eternal Youth.[13] Some would say that this mystical island in the sea is Iona and that the wellspring high on Dun I, Iona's most prominent hill, is the legendary Well of Eternal Youth. When the Hag of Winter sipped from the well, said the legend, she was transformed into the beautiful goddess of spring. She would then raise her hand over the islands, turning them green, and from under her cloak she would scatter snowdrops, the first flowers of spring, across the green fields.

In the Celtic Christian world Brigid becomes the saint of the greening earth and of new life rising. Consequently, she is associated also with the healing energies of the earth and with herbal wisdom. This is part of what we need to reawaken to—the connection between humanity and earth's healing powers, the connection between the spiritual and the physical—in our search for well-being. It will allow us to remember that resurrection energy, the stirring of new life in our souls, and spring energy, the bursting of new life from the earth, come from the same fountain source. The way life rises from the ground is the way new life can come forth from the human soul. Just as we expect spring energy to burst forth from the winter earth every year, so can we faithfully look to what is trying to come forth from the unknown depths of the soul.

What are the barren places within us today, in our lives as individuals, in the most important relationships of life, and in our societies and religious communities? Brigid invites us to remember that there is new life in the belly. We may not know what it will look like, what form and color it might take. We may not know exactly how it is going to come forth or when, but, as surely as we know that new life will emerge from the earth in the spring, we can know that new life is gestating in the soul.

Many stories celebrate the relationship between Brigid and the creatures, both wild and domestic. She is especially associated with cattle and the production of milk, so much so that the St. Brigid's cross can still be found on cowsheds throughout Ireland today. Her name has been invoked over the centuries in milking prayers, sung or chanted in rhythm with the action of milking. May there be "essence in breast . . . substance in udder . . . butter and curd, fat and cheese," says one of the prayers.[14] A portion of another invocation echoes the fourfold rhythm of milking the udder:

The teat of Mary,
The teat of Brigit,
The teat of Michael,
The teat of God.[15]

You will not find such words in the traditional prayer books of Western Christianity. Teats are entirely lacking there, whether creaturely, human, or divine! We need to learn to laugh at this almost unbelievable disconnect between the spiritual and the physical and between the feminine and the divine. If we do not laugh, let us weep, for it is a tragic separation between the realms of grace and nature, a lack of integration that has wreaked havoc in the lives of so many women and men and in humanity's relationship with the earth. But maybe we need to do both, to laugh *and* weep, for both will help release in us holy tears to water the soil of our souls and nurture again our memory of nature's sacredness and the sacredness of the feminine.

It is imperative that we again find ways of living and celebrating this liminality between humanity and the earth, including our creatureliness, for its strands are interwoven inseparably within us. We will be well to the extent that we remember that we are of the earth and remember again to cherish and honor her body. In this time of crisis in humanity's relationship with the earth, as we learn more and more just how deeply we have wronged the earth and how dangerously we are imperiling the future of humanity, we need a reawakening of vision. Brigid will help us in this journey. She will inspire us in reimagining our relationship with the earth, so that we may dream our way forward together into new ways of living and relating.

The fourth threshold is the liminality between the womb and birth. What is trying to emerge from the unseen belly of the universe to manifest among us in new ways at this moment in time?

Because Brigid is said to have been the midwife at the birth of the Christ Child, Brigid myths are infused with birthing symbolism and energy, of helping new life into being. In the Hebrides, when a woman was in labor, the midwife, or "womb woman," as she was called, would go to the door of the house and invoke the presence of Brigid. Part of what this was saying is that the birth of every child is sacred and that the Christ Child is born again and again among us. The marriage of heaven and earth, spirit and matter, time and eternity is happening in the birth of every child and every life-form.

Brigid is spoken of in Hebridean tradition as the "woman on her knees,"[16] a reference not to her posture in prayer, but rather, to her posture in midwifing. Family homes in the Hebrides were usually one-room dwellings. Birth happened at the threshold of the house. This is where the woman in labor could bear down by pushing against the opposite sides of the stone doorway. The expectant mother would be on one knee, hands pressed against the two sides of the threshold, bearing down in labor. The midwife would be on both knees in front of her, assisting in the birth.

Brigid challenges us to be people on our knees, that is, people midwifing new births for this moment in time. The good news is that we do not have to create the births. Our role, rather, is to midwife what is trying to come forth from deep within the human soul.

We live in a threshold moment. We are waking up to the earth again. We are awakening to the feminine and the desire to faithfully tend the interrelationship of all things. In this moment, politically, culturally, and religiously, we are witnessing the death throes of a shadow form of masculine power that has arrayed itself over against the earth and over against the sacredness of the feminine. This shadow form of power, however, has no ultimate future, for it is essentially false in its betrayal of the earth and the feminine. So in fear it is lashing out with unprecedented force. But it is not the deep spirit of this moment in time. Something else is trying to be born.

Just as the earth is forever pushing forth new life, so it is with the human soul. We can be alert to where this is happening, where new vision is trying to be born among us. In other words, we can be watchful for where the waters are breaking.

We come into the world by passing through water. In Celtic wisdom water connects us to the Womb from which all things have come. This is why the shoreline, a liminal place, features in so much Celtic myth and legend. It is the place where land and sea meet, where the soil of our habitation and the primeval waters of our beginnings kiss. It is the meeting place between the known and the unknown, the conscious and the unconscious, the temporal and the eternal.

In the Celtic world all water is sacred, whether the water of the seas or the water of our birth, the water of wells and springs or the water of streams and rivers. Water is part of our genesis and essential to our well-being. Therefore, it must be preserved. For the future of our children and our children's children and for the sake of the earth, the sacredness of water must be protected.

At one time, there were hundreds of wells dedicated to Brigid. There are still many today in Ireland, but not in Scotland. Seventeenth-century Calvinism forbade pilgrimage to holy wells, and the sacred wells of Scotland were either destroyed or blocked up, a tragic symbol of the way the inner well of the soul was also being denied, both individually and collectively. Behind much of this was a fear of the strength of the feminine that Brigid represents. As her father said of her, "She does things without asking permission." When we know that the inner well of our being is sacred, we will serve at that well, we will midwife what is trying to come into consciousness and manifest among us in fresh ways, no matter who tells us not to. There are new beginnings waiting to be born from deep within us. We can serve at these birthings.

Who was this beautiful, wild woman? We need the sacred feminine to be strong again within us, not just in women but also in men, and not just in our individual lives but collectively among us in our communities and nations. The sacred feminine holds great energy for new birthing.

Brigid has lived vibrantly in the Celtic imagination for centuries and, perhaps in a new way, she has been appearing in your soul as you have read these pages, maybe standing at a threshold within you, bathed in light, gazing at you in love to welcome you in. She is emerging again in human consciousness, colorfully calling our attention. This of course is because we need her today, perhaps more than ever before. She is stirring us to be midwife people and threshold communities. She is inspiring us not to be frightened by the pain of labor and the uncertainties of passing through new doorways, but to faithfully serve in this time of fear and transition.

We know next to nothing of Brigid's death, apart from the fact that it is said to have been on February 1, her feast day and the first day of spring, the season of new life rising. One strand of legend says that she died in Glastonbury, which historically was part of a pilgrimage route from Ireland to Jerusalem. According to this legend there was a little chapel close to the cathedral on a hillock, which is still referred to by locals as Little Ireland.

The chapel had an archway that opened from its sanctuary onto nature. It came to be known as Brigid's archway, and it was said that those who passed through it would receive mercy. Brigid leads us into the archway between religion and nature. There she invites us to seek mercy for the wrongs we have done to the earth and to the feminine, that we may find new beginnings.

Near the ruins of this little chapel in Glastonbury is a well dedicated to Brigid, but perhaps the most famous well devoted to Brigid is in Kildare itself. Etched into stone beside it are the words, "Brigid, Mary of the Gaels, pray for us."[17] Let this be our prayer. We need her sacred feminine wisdom at the meeting place of so-called opposites in our lives and world, between spirit and matter, the divine and the human, the masculine and the feminine, humanity and the earth, the life of our nation and the plight of other nations, the insights of our spiritual tradition and the wisdom of other faiths, these and so many more. She will help us in all of these doorways to remember what we deeply know, that the earth and the human soul are sacred.

Brigid, Mary of the Gaels, pray for us.

Brigid is an icon for us today of sacred feminine strength. It is particularly the strength of faithfulness to the interrelationship of all things. This is not a strength that is used *against* another, but *for* one another. It serves our relationship with the earth and the creatures, and it tends our interconnections with those on the other side of boundaries, whether political, racial, or religious. Brigid reminds us that we do not need to wait for permission to be faithful to these sacred interrelationships. We are to act faithfully regardless of the norms and limitations imposed on us by our cultural or religious environments.

What most endangers us as an earth community today is that we have neglected our interrelationships—as countries, faiths, and races. The reality is that we need one another. We will be well to the extent that we all are well. We will be truly strong to the extent that we faithfully protect one another's well-being, not simply the well-being of *our* people, *our* community, or *our* species. The strength of the sacred feminine is deep within us, in both men and women, young and old. It is awakening again in our depths. We need to open to it, now, if we are to be well.

Before concluding this chapter, I invite you to take a few minutes to pay attention to what Brigid has awakened in you. As you do the reflection practice below, sitting in silence, name in gratitude what has been stirring within you from this chapter. (All of the meditative practices are collected in the appendix, which can be used on a daily basis to remain alert to what has been calling your inner attention as you read this book.)

REFLECTION: SACRED FEMININE

WORDS OF AWARENESS

St. Brigid embodies the beauty and strength of the sacred feminine, which is deep within us all. Stories of her life call forth this dimension of the divine in us, that we may be strong again to serve the interrelationship of all things, within us, between us, and among us in the world.

(Reflect for a brief time on the ways this wisdom applies to your life.)

PRAYER OF AWARENESS

Awake, O my soul,
To the beauty of the divine deep within you
And awake to its fragrance in the body of the earth.
Know its strength of attraction
And its grace to heal what has been torn apart.
Awake, O my soul,
To the beauty of the divine deep within you.

(Listen silently for a few minutes within the sacredness of your being.)

Awake, O my soul. Awake.

3

SACRED FLOW:
JOHN SCOTUS ERIUGENA

Celtic wisdom looks for the flow of the divine deep within everything that has being. It is like a subterranean river coursing through the veins of the universe. If somehow it were dammed up or stopped, everything would cease to exist. This sacred flow is not simply a dimension of life that may or may not be there, depending on the moment, the place, the person, or the species. It is the very essence of everything that exists. John Scotus Eriugena awakens us to look for the flow of the divine deep within all things and to release it within ourselves and one another.

In Chapter 1 we explored the life and teachings of Pelagius, the earliest recorded teacher in the Celtic Christian world of Britain. We learned how his vision of earth's sacredness and the sacredness of every human being was a challenge to those in power and how in 418 he was banned by the empire and excommunicated by the church.

At the time of Pelagius's ban, the Roman army had already withdrawn from Britain to stem the barbarian invasions throughout Europe. The Visigoths had sacked Rome in the year 410 under the leadership of King Alaric, thus beginning a separation between imperial Christianity and the Christianity of Celtic Britain that would last for nearly two hundred years. The Celtic tradition was given breathing space in which to develop without the heavy-handed interference of the empire. Pelagius found sanctuary in his homeland of Wales. The Celtic way of seeing was safe and, for the time being, flourished. Its vision of the sacredness of the earth and every human being continued unhindered.

A contemporary of Pelagius's was St. Patrick (ca. 385–461). Although Patrick was trained by the Roman church in Gaul and thus is not as pure an expression of the Celtic tradition as Pelagius and Brigid, the prayer that was attributed to him in later centuries is typical of the Celtic vision of the interweaving of spirit and matter and the seeking of the divine within the naturalness of the physical world. The prayer, known as *The Breastplate Hymn of St. Patrick*, is part of the tradition of protection prayers in the Celtic world. It is also called *The Lorica of St. Patrick* or *The Deer's Cry*.

The hymn begins by invoking the protection of the Trinity: "I bind unto myself today the strong name of the Trinity."[1] The next verse calls on the guardianship of Christ: "I bind unto myself for ever Christ's Incarnation." In the third verse the angelic realm and the enfolding of those who have gone before us are invoked: "I bind unto myself this day the love of angels and of saints." The fourth verse then takes us from the heavenly sphere, both divine and angelic, to earth's graces of protection, invoking the elemental forces of earth, air, fire, and water—a celebration of the sacred energies that flow deep in the body of the universe:

> *I bind unto myself today*
> *The virtues of the star-lit heaven,*
> *The glorious sun's life-giving rays,*
> *The whiteness of the moon at even,*
> *The flashing of the lightning free,*
> *The whirling winds tempestuous shocks,*
> *The stable earth, the deep salt sea*
> *Around the old eternal rocks.*

A more literal translation of the ancient Irish text reads:

> *I bind to myself today*
> *The energy of stars,*
> *The brilliance of sun,*
> *The whiteness of moon,*
> *The splendor of fire,*
> *The flashing of lightning,*
> *The wildness of wind,*

The depth of seas,
The fecundity of earth,
The solidity of rocks.

The hymn invokes not simply the transcendent aspects of grace, but also its immanent elemental energies. It is interesting to note that this fourth verse, in which the graces of nature are invoked, is entirely omitted (or asterisked as optional) in many Western Christian hymnbooks. This reflects the tragic separation between grace and nature, between the spiritual and the physical, that has dominated so much of our Western Christian inheritance and made room for the Western world's unchecked exploitation and abuse of nature. We urgently need to awaken again to the reintegration of the spiritual and the physical, if we are to begin to reverse the threat to planetary existence as we have known it.

The fifth and sixth centuries were like a golden age in Celtic Christianity, in which the teachings and vision of prophets like Pelagius and Brigid thrived. The golden age was cut short, however, in 597 with the arrival of the imperial Christian mission in Britain. The two-hundred-year breathing space was over, and its vision of the sacredness of the earth and every human being was about to come under siege.

The mission from Rome was led by a priest named Augustine, later known as Augustine of Canterbury, namesake of the fourth-century Augustine of Hippo. He arrived in Britain with the authority of the empire and promptly summoned the Celtic leaders to a meeting. His intention was to demand uniformity with the Roman church and its alliance with imperial power.

The Celtic leaders were uncertain whether they should agree to the meeting and pay heed to Augustine's demands. So they sought the advice of a wise old hermit monk who told them that, if Augustine was a man of God, they should agree to meet with him and listen to him.

"But how can we know if he is a man of God?" they asked.

The monk replied, "If he is a humble man, then you can know that he is a man of God."

"But how can we know even this?" they continued.

So the old monk advised them: "Arrange that Augustine and his followers arrive first at the place appointed for the conference. If he rises courteously as you approach, rest assured that he is the servant of Christ and do as he asks. But if he ignores you and does not rise, then do not comply with his demands."[2]

Accordingly, the Celtic leaders arrived late at the great oak tree in Gloucestershire, where the meeting was to take place. Augustine was already seated and, as they approached, he did not rise to greet them. Instead, as the account says, Augustine in his "pride" refused to stand. The stage was set for a clash that would hold tragic implications for the Western world in its relationship with the earth and its lack of regard for the feminine and the essential sacredness of every human being.

The differences between these two streams of Christianity were enormous. Over the two-hundred-year period of separation, the imperial church had increasingly accentuated the doctrine of original sin in its teachings and practices. On the other hand, the Celtic church, like the Eastern Orthodox tradition, had continued to celebrate that what is deepest in the newborn child, and thus at the heart of every woman and man, is the dignity of the divine. Also, the imperial church over this time had imposed celibacy as the required norm for priesthood, whereas the Celtic church continued the practice of priestly marriage, with the option of celibacy in monastic life. In addition to these significant differences, the Roman tradition had firmly subordinated the place of women, whereas the Celtic tradition was characterized by both male and female leadership, as the feminine and the masculine were regarded equally as sacred manifestations of the divine.

There were also significant differences in structure. The imperial church was hierarchical. The bishop of Rome imposed uniformity from above in matters of faith and practice. The Celtic church, on the other hand, had no single center of authority. It was a federation of monastic communities, enjoying considerable independence among its members and unique expressions of faith. A good example of this can be found in the monastic community of St. Columba on Iona. Uniquely its rule of monastic life instructed the monks of Iona to "Pray until the tears come."[3]

"Pray until the tears come"—this unparalleled sixth-century practice of prayer, although almost entirely forgotten now, has continued, over the centuries, to bless Iona and the countless numbers of pilgrims who have journeyed to this island. During my time of leadership at the abbey and in the many years since then of leading international pilgrimage weeks, I have met people from all over the world who have experienced a flow of tears on Iona. For some the tears come unexpectedly, even as they first step onto the island. For others it is after days and nights of reflection that their hearts open to a deep flow of feeling. Carl Jung says, when we weep, something in the salt sea of life's origins is stirring in us again. We are awakening to a flow at the very heart of our being.

In so much of our Western culture and religion we have been frightened, even ashamed, of tears, as if what they primarily reveal in us is emotional weakness or lack of self-control. But Iona teaches us that tears can cleanse our inner sight, washing the lens of the heart, that we may see clearly again the glistening of heaven in earth and also feel more deeply within us the current of life's sorrows. Tears can be a transformative part of the journey toward wholeness.

One of the most striking examples of difference between the Celtic tradition and the Roman is found in their distinct approaches to human sexuality. We have a detailed record of correspondence between Augustine of Canterbury and Pope Gregory on this matter, focusing on three principal questions from Augustine. Augustine first asked, "May a woman . . . enter church at the time of menstruation? And may she receive Communion at these times?" adding, "These uncouth people require guidance on all these matters."[4] The pope replied by saying that, although menstruation in women is a "defilement," it is not exactly their fault, so they should not be barred from entering church during their menstrual cycle. But if, out of consideration for the sacrament, they do not "presume" to receive the bread and the wine, then they are to be commended for their restraint.

Augustine's second question was whether a man should be allowed to enter church after he has sexually known his wife. The pope responded, "It is not fitting that a man who has approached his wife should enter church before he has washed. . . . Nor is he to enter the church . . . until the heat of his desire has cooled." The pope proceeded to say that sexual union between husband and wife was not in and of itself the problem. The problem was desire for sexual union. "The fault lies in the bodily pleasure," he said. Intercourse should only be for procreation, for producing offspring.

The teachings of the church, he concluded, give husband and wife "permission" to have sexual relations, but this permission carries a "warning" with it, namely, to avoid taking pleasure in the act.

The third question was, "May a man receive Communion after a sexual illusion in a dream?" In response the pope said that it depended on whether the dream had arisen from "overeating" or "impure thoughts." It became a problem only if the man proceeded to "take pleasure in it" or "consented" to the dream.

If one is in any doubt about the beginnings of sexual confusion in Western Christianity, and thus in so much of Western society and culture, one has only to read this correspondence between Augustine and Pope Gregory to see how the theology of the Roman tradition played a significant part. It has caused countless numbers of men and women to feel ashamed or guilt-ridden about their sexual energies. It has also laid the groundwork for the tragic combination that we witness today in which a lack of radical affirmation of human sexuality's sacredness has paved the way for the objectification of the body and sexual abuse, including the abuses that have happened behind the closed doors of religious authority.

The golden age of Celtic Christianity in Britain was over, and a major clash with imperial Christianity had begun.

The conflict grew over the next century, coming to a head in the kingdom of Northumbria. Oswy, the king, had been schooled on

Iona, whereas his wife, Eanflada, had been educated in the south under the influence of the Roman mission. In the royal court the conflict expressed itself through the different dating of Easter that had developed in the respective churches during their time of separation.

The Celtic dating of Easter had been influenced by the tradition of the disciple John the Beloved, a favorite figure in Celtic legend. In his community, in Asia Minor, Easter had been celebrated on the night of the first full moon after the spring equinox. It was believed that this is when the resurrection of Christ had occurred.

The Roman dating of Easter, on the other hand, was the Sunday following the first full moon after the spring equinox. This accommodated the celebration of Easter to the liturgical practices of the church and its Sunday observances. Thus, Easter's relationship to the moon's light and to the natural cycle of the seasons had increasingly been obscured.

To celebrate Easter under the full moon, its round whiteness glowing in the night sky, is to more readily remember the promise of the universe, that out of darkness comes light and that this light can grow into perfect fullness. In the intimacy of the night, gathered with others around a blazing fire, we are assured by the heavens of what we sense in our hearts, that new beginnings can grow out of seasons of darkness and death. We can know the connection between nature and grace, between the movement of the spheres above and our inner landscape of soul, and we can imagine fully awakening to the sacredness of the universe and one another again. It is in such faithful imagining together that we will help bring about what we are most deeply longing for, a resurrection of harmony in our lives and world.

The difference in the dating of Easter meant that the court in Northumbria needed to have two celebrations of Easter most years, one for the king and one for the queen. Oswy decided to convene a synod to deal with the conflict, for it was affecting not only the court but the entire kingdom. The synod met at Whitby in the year 664 at a Celtic double monastery of men and women living under the leadership of the abbess Hilda.

Ostensibly the synod was convened to address two basic issues that separated the Roman and Celtic practices, the dating of Easter and the clerical tonsure. As we have already noted in Chapter 1, there was a difference between the Roman tonsure and the Celtic tonsure, the latter based on the pre-Christian Druidic tonsure. But the conflict was much more than a difference of calendar and hairstyle—it was a clash between two radically different ways of seeing.

The monk Colman of Iona was appointed to speak on behalf of the Celtic tradition. He appealed to the authority of John, the disciple who leaned against Jesus at the Last Supper. Wilfrid, on the other hand, the spokesman for the imperial church, appealed to the authority of Peter, remembering him especially as the disciple to whom Jesus had entrusted the keys of the kingdom of heaven. Wilfrid argued that the Roman custom of dating Easter was the norm throughout the world. The only people "who stupidly contend" against the rest of the world on this, he said, are these Celts.[5]

Oswy in the end was swayed by the arguments of the Roman tradition, likely seduced by its power and the outward authority of the empire. But the conflict was not so easily resolved beyond the borders of the realm of Northumbria. The Celtic church as a whole had no single center of authority. It needed therefore to be conquered in segments.

In 686, over twenty years after the Synod of Whitby, Adamnan, the abbot of Iona, visited Lindisfarne. There he acquiesced to the decree of Whitby and conformed to the practices of the Roman church. But when he returned to Iona wearing the Roman tonsure, his monastic community rejected his leadership. And for centuries to come Iona would resist the decision of Whitby.

Christianity in Scotland remained essentially Celtic until the twelfth century, five hundred years after the judgment of Whitby. This was the pattern also in Wales, Cornwall, and parts of Ireland. In the twelfth century, however, Benedictine abbeys began to replace the great Celtic monastic sites, a move by the Roman church to enforce uniformity in Britain and Ireland. The message to the remaining Celtic monks in these historic locations, such as Iona, was, "Conform or get out."

Many of those who got out were Culdees, a term derived from

the Gaelic *céilí Dé*, meaning "companions of God." They lived a monastic life without taking formal vows, which meant that they remained relatively free from ecclesiastical control. For centuries to come it was itinerant Culdees, wandering teachers, who helped keep alive in the people the threatened vision of their ancient Celtic inheritance and its sense of the sacredness of the earth and all people.

But the five-hundred-year period of resistance to the decree of Whitby had also been a time of immense creativity, both spiritually and artistically. It was during these centuries that the high-standing crosses of the Celtic world came to their peak of artistic expression. Sometimes more than twenty feet in height, these often richly decorated carved stone crosses reflect the Celtic practice of worship outside in the great cathedral of earth, sea, and sky, as it was called. These magnificent stone structures, planted deep in the earth, pointed to the connection between grace and nature, spirit and matter, heaven and earth.

Typically, the Celtic cross design consists of two conjoined symbols. The first is the symbol of Christ, represented by the cross form. The second is the symbol of the cosmos, perhaps also a sun image, represented by the circle that overlays the cross. Both symbols are centered on the intersection of the vertical and horizontal shafts of the cross. Thus, Celtic art speaks of Christ and the cosmos coming forth from the same point of origin. The deeper we move into the Christ mystery, the closer we come to the true heart of all life. The deeper we move in anything that has being, the closer we come to the presence that Christ embodies. The sacred was seen as the very heart of all things.

The high crosses were also typically decorated with the sculpted knot work and interlacing patterns that characterize Celtic art generally, especially in its sophisticated silversmithing and brilliantly illuminated manuscripts. This interlacing design, in which one strand is so deftly interwoven with the other that it is impossible to see where the one begins and the other ends, has sometimes been called the "everlasting pattern." The vision is of time and eternity intertwined, heaven and earth inseparably woven together, the sacred forever flowing deep in the matter of earth and the human mystery.

Also, in the five-hundred-year period of resistance, there had been considerable Celtic influence on mainland Europe. We spoke earlier of the figure of the *scotus vagans*, or wandering Irish teacher. Hundreds of these wandering scholars now roamed Europe in the wake of the Norse invasions into Ireland and northern Scotland. These *peregrini*, as they were also known, viewed their wanderings, or peregrinations, as a process of seeking their place of "resurrection"—they were searching for their path of new beginnings.[6] And this they often found in monasteries and other centers of learning throughout Europe. These "merchants of wisdom," as they described themselves, were scholars, not priests, and thus less bound by ecclesiastical control.[7]

Their presence in mainland Europe worried the imperial church, for they were not ecclesiastically accountable to the bishops. The Council of Mainz, in 813, described them as monstrous creatures beyond control by church authorities. Celtic wisdom may have been denied a place theologically in the teachings of the church, but the wandering scholars now gave it philosophical form in some of Europe's principal schools of thought and study. The vision of the sacredness of the earth and the human soul was finding its place of resurrection.

Perhaps the greatest of these wandering scholars was John Scotus Eriugena (ca. 815–77). After leaving Ireland, he became in time the head of the palace school of Charles, king of France, at Aachen in Gaul. Eriugena's vision was not so much a theology as a cosmology of the sacred. God, he said, is the "essence of all things."[8]

For Eriugena, the Light of the divine is like a subterranean river flowing through the body of the earth and of everything that has being. He interpreted the Greek word for God, *theos*, as being derived from the Greek verb, *theo*, which means "to flow or run." God is the flow of life deep in all things. Everything, he said, is essentially a "theophany," a showing of the divine.[9] We are "gods," he says, "made from God."[10] The deeper we move in any created thing, the closer we come to the "divine brilliance" from which all life flows.[11] Every life-form reveals God, or, as the earlier Irish wandering scholar Columbanus had said, if we wish to know the Creator, let us come to know the creatures.

Years ago, during an Iona pilgrimage week, I shared an evening meal with a woman from Florida who was about seventy years of age. During dinner she recounted to me her spiritual journey and, in particular, something that had happened to her over fifty-five years earlier when she was an adolescent girl in church one Sunday with her family. Halfway through the service a dog wandered into the sanctuary and sauntered up the central aisle. When it approached the front of the church, it began to sniff around the altar. But then it chose to leave. "It didn't like what it smelled," she said. "It didn't smell right. It didn't smell natural." The young girl got up and followed the dog out of the church, never to return.

This woman's story is eccentric in some of its details. At another level, however, it is the story of hundreds of thousands of our brothers and sisters who began life in the Christian household, but who do not return to the family table to be fed because something doesn't "smell right." It doesn't smell natural.

This woman did not tell her story with pride. She wasn't apologetic about her instinct for the sacredness of the natural, but at the same time there was a sadness in her story, because for over half a century she had lived without a community with whom to pray. She did not have others with whom to religiously celebrate moments of joy and new life or to mourn at times of loss and grief. She did not have the benefit of a spiritual network to help her work for transformation in the world. In this also, I believe, she is not alone. Countless numbers of our brothers and sisters who live in exile from their spiritual family of birth are also lonely, and many of them too are longing for a new vision of the sacred around which to gather again.

Why did this woman come to Iona? I think she sensed that her story would be understood in the Celtic world. I think she also came searching for community, not necessarily a local community with which she could gather on a regular basis, as important and even vital as that form of community is. What this woman was primarily looking for was a community of men and women who shared her sense of the sacredness of the natural, and thus her desire to see that what happens in a church building should reflect the sacredness of nature. The more those who are in exile are able to find each other or existing communities on the ground that share their yearnings, the more likely it is that new expressions of this ancient vision will be born again among us in community.

Shortly after meeting this woman on Iona, I was telling her story during a morning presentation at St Patrick's Cathedral in Armagh. In the afternoon I invited the participants to go outside and allow their instinct for the sacredness of the earth to speak to them. This they did. But what I had failed to notice upon entering the cathedral grounds that morning was that all around the cathedral there were signs that read "No Dogs Allowed."

What is this fear of the creatures? And, indeed, what is this fear of the creaturely within us?

Eriugena said that the whole of the natural world is like a sacred text—and that includes the creatures and our creatureliness. "All creatures," he says, "are in humanity as if melted down in a crucible."[12] Eriugena teaches that there are two books through which God is speaking. The first is the small book; physically little, this is the book of Holy Scripture. The second is the big book, the living text of the universe, which includes the great luminaries of the heavens, the sun, moon, and stars; the earth, sea, and sky; the creatures of all these realms; and the multiplicity of life-forms that grow from the ground. We need to read both books, he says, the sacred text of scripture *and* the sacred text of the universe. If we read only the little book, we will miss the vastness and wildness of the utterance, everything vibrating with the sound of the divine. If we read only the big book, we are in danger of missing the intimacy of the voice, for the book of scripture calls us to faithfulness in relationship, including faithfulness to strangers, refugees, widows, and the poorest among us.

Everything is sacred, says Eriugena, but we live in a state of forgetfulness of what is deepest in us and in everything that has being. The more we forget our true identity, the less we treat one another as sacred. We suffer from "soul-forgetfulness." But Christ, he says, is our memory, our "epiphany."[13] He comes to show us what we have forgotten, that we are bearers of the divine flow. He re-awakens us to our true nature and the true nature of the earth, that we and all things are in essence sacred.

In the Celtic world Christ is viewed not as coming to reveal a foreign truth, but to disclose the deepest truth of our being. The word *revelation* is derived from the Latin *revelare*, which means "to lift the veil." Christ is viewed as lifting the veil that we may see again who we are, made of God, and that we may know again the sacred essence of the earth and of everything that has being.

Eriugena looks for the divine Light everywhere and in everyone. He even refers to the Satan figure in scripture as Lucifer, which means "Angel of Light." For Eriugena, Satan is false to the extent that he is not being truly himself. He is an archetype of the false self, living in shadow and in exile from his true center. But Eriugena believes that Satan in the end will return to himself, for at the heart of his being, and at the heart of all being, is the light that the darkness has not overcome. Eriugena offers us hope even where the sacred has been denied or covered over in our lives or world. It has not been undone. It is waiting to rise again.

We are being invited to call others by their true name, to view them in their deepest identity, to see and think of them not primarily for their failings, but first and foremost in their original nature, made of God. Each one of us is essentially brother of Light, sister of Light, no matter what we have done, even those in whom there appears to be only falseness and violence. At the heart of our being is the light from which we have come. We can choose to live from this place of deepest identity and, at the same time, confront the darkness that violates the light in ourselves and one another. We can call each other back to live from these true depths, not because we have somehow achieved sacredness in our lives, but because we are made of sacredness, pure grace.

Sin or evil leads to a "deformity" of our true countenance, says Eriugena. It is like a "leprosy of soul."[14] Our face becomes distorted, even monstrous, in appearance. Like leprosy, sin is essentially a disease of insensitivity or loss of feeling. We become numb to the sacred within ourselves and one another, and we become false and destructive in our actions. But this is not our true nature. This is when we are being untrue to ourselves, one another, and the earth. We need the "medicine of grace," says Eriugena, to heal our nature and free us from the ugliness of what we have done, that our true countenance may shine forth again.[15]

Nature is the "gift of being," says Eriugena, and it is a sacred gift. Grace, on the other hand, is the "gift of well-being,"[16] given not to change the heart of our nature, but to release the true heart of our nature. Nature "forms" us, he says, and grace "reforms" us.[17] In the Gospel story of Jesus healing the lepers, the lepers are not given new faces, says Eriugena. Rather, they are restored to their true faces. The medicine of grace is given not to banish our nature, but to awaken us to our nature, made of God.

When someone has made a mistake or been untrue, we often say, "Well, that's just human nature." But in Celtic wisdom these actions are not viewed as human nature. They are a betrayal of our nature, a denial of what is deepest in us, the sacred essence of the divine. The invitation is not to become something other than ourselves. It is to become truly ourselves.

Eriugena, like Pelagius, was a threat to imperial Christianity. There were big implications to seeing that everything is essentially sacred. The empire would have to change its ways. Consequently, Eriugena's writings were condemned by two church councils, the first in 855 and the second in 859. The former described his work as "Scot's porridge," interestingly echoing Jerome's criticism of Pelagius in the fifth century. The second council described his writings as "old women's stories," a revealing choice of words that expresses both a fear of the feminine and a disregard for the imagination, both of which were cherished in the Celtic world.[18]

After the condemnation of his works in 859, Eriugena was summoned to Rome to be disciplined for his teachings. But his benefactor, King Charles, advised against his going and provided Eriugena with sanctuary in the French court. He died in 877, not at the hands of Rome, but peacefully, it seems, in Gaul. One strand of legend, however, claims that students stabbed Eriugena to death with their pens. But this story likely reflects how academics treated him after his death rather than the actual cause of his death. In later centuries, the Vatican and its theologians tried again and again to assassinate his character and prevent his writings from being read, but Eriugena's voice could not be silenced.

In 1225, nearly three hundred and fifty years after his death, his works were condemned once more, as "swarming with worms."[19] In 1585, almost seven hundred years after his death, he was yet again judged in a papal encyclical and his writings forbidden. But Eriugena would not have been bothered by this judgment, because for him the pope held no monopoly on the truth. Each one of us, he believed, has access to the well of wisdom. Its source flows deep in all things. It is not the property of religion. It is the birthright of all.

Eriugena, as a ninth-century *peregrinus*, had found his place of resurrection in the palace school at Aachen, in France. Similarly, his words and wisdom are coming to birth among us again today. His words are resonating with the quest of the modern soul, as our instinct to find the sacredness in earth and nature is rising again. Anything else does not smell right. A new generation of *peregrini* is emerging. For countless numbers of men and women today the traditional formulations of imperial Christianity have died. Thirty-five percent of millennials in America, for instance, have no religious affiliation whatsoever.[20] They are part of a new wave of spiritual seekers, and for many it is the resurrection of an ancient vision of the sacred flow that runs deep in the body of the earth and in everything that has being. It is a new-ancient vision, calling us not only to awaken to this sacredness but to protect this sacredness, for it is the essence of our life. It is the essence of all life.

Eriugena is an icon for us today as we seek the flow of the divine in all things. He offers a wisdom that is grounded in both the human soul and the soil of the earth. He sees that spiritual truth and physical truth are one. The energies that stir in our depths are also the forces that move the planets. The microcosm and the macrocosm are expressions of the same sacred reality. The part and the whole are forever intertwined. Truth is both intimate and immense, personal and vast. Thus, wisdom is always unitive, seeking the oneness and interrelatedness that underlies all things. As Eriugena says, God is the essence of *all* things.

Part of what Eriugena's wisdom can foster in us for today is a strong sense of inner authority in a time of immense outward transition and change. To look for the flow of the divine in all things is not to disregard the external authorities of religion, nation, or culture. But it is always to consult also the compass of the soul and our place of inner knowing. So often we have been given the impression that faith primarily means accepting doctrinal beliefs or precepts that have been dispensed from above. Religious leaders appeal to scripture or the prerogative of tradition, often forgetting that these outward authorities need to be read and appraised through the lens of our inner knowing and the deepest experiences of our lives in relation to the earth and one another.

If we are to see a true reawakening to the sacredness of the earth and harness the deepest energies of our being to serve this awareness, we need a strong inner authority in our own souls to challenge the religious, political, and social systems that have recklessly ignored or denied this sacredness and are imperiling the very future of the world. Our capacity to know the flow of the divine in all things, pure gift of God, is deep within us; we only need to access it together for the great challenges of this moment in time.

Before concluding this chapter, I invite you to take a few minutes to pay attention to what Eriugena has awakened in you. As you do the reflection practice below, sitting in silence, name in gratitude what has been stirring within you from this chapter. (All of the meditative practices are collected in the appendix, which can be used on a daily basis to remain alert to what has been calling your inner attention as you read this book.)

REFLECTION: SACRED FLOW

WORDS OF AWARENESS

John Scotus Eriugena sees the divine as a subterranean river flowing through the body of the earth and through everything that has being. This sacred river runs also through you and through me. We can open to it now to be more fully alive.

(*Reflect for a brief time on the ways this wisdom applies to your life.*)

PRAYER OF AWARENESS

Awake, O my soul,
To the flow of the divine deep within you.
Awake to it in every creature, in every woman, in every man.
It is our river of resurrection, the promise of new beginnings.
Awake, O my soul,
To the flow of the divine deep within you.

(*Listen silently for a few minutes within the sacredness of your being.*)

Awake, O my soul. Awake.

SACRED SONG:
THE CARMINA GADELICA

In the Celtic world, it is poetry that has most powerfully expressed the wisdom of the human soul over the centuries. In times of loss and adversity it is the song of the soul that has safeguarded a memory of life's sacredness and a belief in love's graces:

> *Grace of the love of the skies be thine,*
> *Grace of the love of the stars be thine,*
> *Grace of the love of the moon be thine,*
> *Grace of the love of the sun be thine.*[1]

These words come down to us in an ancient stream of prayer from the western islands of Scotland. It is thought that some of them date back to the sixth-century community of St. Columba on the isle of Iona and even before Christianity to Eastern influences on the Celtic world. They were passed down in the oral tradition, chanted and sung by men and women at the rising of the sun and its setting or at the birth of a child and the death of a loved one. They belong not so much to formal religion as to life in the sacredness of nature, or to what the Celts called the cathedral of earth, sea, and sky. They belong to the changing of the seasons, the ebbing and flowing of the tides, the waxing and waning of the moon. In being accessed anew today, they can help reawaken in us the desire to live in relation to the sacredness of the earth and the human soul.

Many of these poems and songs were collected in the nineteenth century by Alexander Carmichael (1832–1912). Born on the island of Lismore, in the Inner Hebrides, he spent most of his life in the islands. As an excise man traveling extensively throughout the Hebrides, he was able over the decades to make a vast collection of the songs and prayers of the people. He transcribed them from the spoken Gaelic, translated them into English, and in 1900 began to publish them under the title *Carmina Gadelica* ("The Songs of the Gaels").

In these prayers, earth, air, fire, and water are seen as sacred, and the life-giving energies of the divine are viewed as both encompassing and interpenetrating the human:

> *God to enfold me,*
> *God to surround me,*
> *God in my speaking,*
> *God in my thinking.*

God in my sleeping,
God in my waking,
God in my watching,
God in my hoping.

God in my life,
God in my lips,
God in my hands,
God in my heart.[2]

Many of these blessings were considered by their critics to be pagan in origin, which is probably true! But this makes them richer, not poorer. They carry pre-Christian wisdom into a Christian expression of faith. The Gaelic spoken in the Hebrides of Scotland is related to Sanskrit, and something of ancient India's sense of the sacred universe can be heard again and again in these prayers. The Celtic world's path of descent from the East is obscured in the mists of prehistory, but linguistically the commonalities are clear. These Gaelic prayers echo the East's vision of a natural world that breathes with spirit.

In the *Carmina Gadelica* collection, there is the story of a woman from the island of Harris who suffered a type of skin disease and was required to live alone on the shore. There she collected birds' eggs, fish, and seaweed. After boiling them in water and eating them, she would bathe her sores in the remaining liquid. In time she was healed and saw that her healing had come through the elements of earth, sea, and sky. Carmichael records a prayer attributed to her:

> *There is no plant in the ground*
> *But is full of . . . [God's] virtue,*
> *There is no form in the strand*
> *But is full of His blessing. . . .*
>
> *There is no life in the sea,*
> *There is no creature in the river, . . .*
> *There is no bird on the wing,*
> *There is no star in the sky,*
> *There is nothing beneath the sun,*
> *But proclaims His goodness.*[3]

Everything was seen as a manifestation of God in which the energies of the divine flowed. Heaven and earth were interwoven, Christ was Son of Heaven and also Son of Earth, Son of the Moon, Son of the Seas, Son of the Storm. The elements were sacred, and sun and moon were reverenced. As Mor MacNeill, a woman from Barra, told Carmichael:

> *In the time of my father and my mother there was no man in*
> *Barra who would not take off his bonnet to the white sun of*
> *power, nor a woman in Barra who would not bend her body*

to the white moon of the seasons. No, my dear, not a man nor
a woman in Barra. And old persons will be doing this still,
and I will be doing it myself sometimes.[4]

As one of the ancient songs, recited especially by women, expresses it:

When I see the new moon,
It becomes me to lift mine eye,
It becomes me to bend my knee,
It becomes me to bow my head.[5]

Just as women bowed to the moon at night, so men at the beginning of the day would take off their caps to the rising sun, reverencing the Light that is within all light, the Sun that is behind all suns:

The eye of the great God,
The eye of the God of glory . . .
Pouring upon us
At each time and season,
Pouring upon us
Gently and generously.

Glory to thee,
Thou glorious sun.

Glory to thee, thou sun,
Face of the God of life.[6]

These were the songs of men and women reverencing the lights of the skies and alive to nature's rhythms and seasons.

People often went to the shore to pray, sometimes walking for miles to reach the sea, to join their voice to what was called "the voicing of the waves . . . the praises of the ceaseless sea."[7] The shoreline, that liminal space between land and sea, between the known and unknown, the soil of our habitation and the waters of life's origins, was a portal that opened to the union of the temporal and the eternal, the seen and the unseen.

But every place was viewed as a convergence of time and eternity, heaven and earth. As a young woman from Moydart, Catherine Maclennan, said to Carmichael:

My mother would be asking us to sing our morning song to God down in the . . . [garden], as Mary's lark was singing up in the clouds, and as Christ's mavis was singing it yonder in the tree, giving glory to the God of the creatures for the repose of the night, for the light of day, and for the joy of life. She would tell us that every creature on the earth here below and in the ocean beneath and in the air above was giving glory to the great God of the creatures and the worlds, of the virtues and the blessings, and would we be dumb![8]

This was a reverencing of the mystery deeply present in all things, the divine and the human intermingled, spirit and matter conjoined. Consequently, Christ's birth was celebrated not as the coming of a light that was foreign to the earth, but as a manifestation of the light that is in the earth, the light that is in the sea, the light that is in the sky.

In a Christmas carol sung to Carmichael by Roderick Mac-Neill, of Barra, it was said that the earth glowed to the Christ Child at his birth:

This night is the long night,
It will snow and it will drift,
White snow there will be till day,
White snow there will be till morn.
This night is the eve of the Great Nativity,
This night is born to us Mary's Son, . . .
This night is born to us the root of our joy.
This night gleamed the sun of the mountains high,
This night gleamed sea and shore together, . . .
Ere 'twas heard that his foot had reached the earth,
Heard was the song of the angels glorious,
This night is the long night.

Glowed to him wood and tree,
Glowed to him mount and sea,

Glowed to him land and plain,
When that his foot was come to earth.[9]

The light that was in the earth, the light that was in the sea, the light that was in the sky danced with the light that was in the Child, born of heaven, born of earth.

The Christmas carol speaks of what is true of every birth, every child and life-form, a fresh coming of the divine among us. So the "womb women" (midwives) would bless the newborn child as sacred. The midwife Peggy MacCormack told Carmichael:

When the image of the God of life is born into the world, I put
three little drops of water on the child's forehead, [saying:]

"The little drop of the Father
On thy little forehead, beloved one.

The little drop of the Son
On thy little forehead, beloved one.

The little drop of the Spirit
On thy little forehead, beloved one. . . .

To keep thee for the Three,
To shield thee, to surround thee,

To save thee for the Three,
To fill thee with the graces,

The little drop of the Three
To lave [bathe] thee with the graces."[10]

As the birth of the Christ Child was acclaimed by angelic song, ". . . on earth peace, goodwill among people" (Luke 2:14), so the Christhood of every child, of every man and woman, was destined for the work of peace. To know the sacred essence of our being is to know also our calling to serve this sacredness in one another and in the relationships of our lives and world:

Peace between neighbors,
Peace between kindred,
Peace between lovers,
In love of the King of life.

Peace between person and person,
Peace between wife and husband,
Peace between woman and children,
The peace of Christ above all peace.

Bless, O Christ, my face,
Let my face bless everything;

Bless, O Christ, mine eye,
Let mine eye bless all it sees.[11]

Peace, well-being, and blessing were sought not only for those known and loved, but also for the "other"—travelers, foreigners, strangers. These too are sacred. In an ancient Celtic rune of hospitality, attributed originally to St. Brigid, it is said:

We saw a stranger yesterday.
We put food in the eating place,
drink in the drinking place,
music in the listening place,
and, with the sacred name of the triune God,
he blessed us and our house,
our cattle and our dear ones.
As the lark says in her song,
"Often, often, often, goes Christ in the stranger's guise."[12]

Here Christ is seen not only in the heart of the other, but in the body of the other—thus food in the eating place, drink in the drinking place, music in the listening place. The soul was viewed not as merely inhabiting the body, but as entirely suffusing the body; the physical was imbued with the spiritual.

This opened the door in the Celtic world to seeing the sacredness of physical relationship and human sexuality. To touch the body of another in the mutuality of self-giving love is to know the divine in the intimacy of human form. Dugall MacAulay, of Ben-becula, said to Carmichael that when he went to bed at night he would pray:

> *Bless to me the bed-companion of my love,*
> *Bless to me the handling of my hands, . . .*
> *Bless to me, O bless to me the angeling of my rest.*[13]

Also, as Isobel, the fifteenth-century Duchess of Argyll, earnestly prayed:

> *There is a youth comes wooing me,*
> *O King of kings, may he succeed!*
> *Would that he were stretched upon my breast,*
> *With his body against my skin.*[14]

The human soul and the human body were sacred, so dancing and desiring and loving were honored.

And just as birth and life and loving were celebrated as sacred, so the journey of death was viewed as holy. It was a voyage into the heart of nature, a returning to God. Death was spoken of as "the river hard to see." It is hard to see because we do not know when we will have to enter it, hard to see because we fear entering it. But waiting on the other side of death's waters are the midwives of eternity, or what the prayers call "the sainted women of heaven," waiting with outstretched arms to receive us. We may fear entering the cold waters of our mortality, but in the Celtic world there is the hope that, just as the newborn child is received with love through the waters of birth, so upon death's crossing we are welcomed back to the place of our beginnings:

> *Be each saint in heaven,*
> *Each sainted woman in heaven,*
> *Each angel in heaven,*
> *Stretching their arms for you,*
> *Smoothing the way for you,*
> *When you go thither*
> *Over the river hard to see,*
> *Oh when you go thither home*
> *Over the river hard to see.*[15]

At the deathbed of a loved one, prayers were chanted, peace sought, and ancient blessings intoned. Death was the final journey to the home of the seasons:

> *Thou goest home this night to thy home of winter,*
> *To thy home of autumn, of spring, and of summer;*
> *Thou goest home this night to thy perpetual home,*
> *To thine eternal bed, to thine eternal slumber.*
>
> *Sleep thou, sleep, and away with thy sorrow, . . .*
> *Sleep this night in the breast of thy Mother,*

Sleep, thou beloved, while she herself soothes thee, . . .
Sleep, thou beloved, while she herself kisses thee.

The great sleep of Jesus, the surpassing sleep of Jesus,
The sleep of Jesus' wound, the sleep of Jesus' grief,
The young sleep of Jesus, the restoring sleep of Jesus,
The sleep of the kiss of Jesus of peace and of glory. . . .

Sleep, O sleep in the calm of all calm,
Sleep, O sleep in the guidance of guidance,
Sleep, O sleep in the love of all loves, . . .
Sleep, O beloved, in the God of life.[16]

What happened to this spirituality that saw the universe as sacred and Christhood in every newborn child? That wove together heaven and earth, flesh and angels, prayer and nature? And why is it that this way of seeing was lost in so much of our Western Christian inheritance? Formal opposition began in the sixteenth century with the Scottish Reformation, which saw Celtic prayers as little better than pagan practices. Opposition intensified in the seventeenth and eighteenth centuries when Calvinism denounced Celtic teachings as "lying Gaelic stories."[17] Prudish legalism now began to replace the life-affirming spirituality of the islands. Even the rooster was locked away on the Sabbath, lest it think of doing anything "natural" with the hens!

On the island of Lewis, Carmichael asked a local woman if there was still music, dancing, and singing at wedding feasts:

> *Oh, indeed, no, our weddings are now quiet and becoming, not the foolish things they were in my young days. . . . In my young days there was hardly a house in Ness in which there was not one or two or three who could play the pipe or the fiddle. . . . A blessed change came over the place and the people, and the good men and the good ministers who arose did away with the songs and the stories, the music and the dancing, the sports and the games, that were perverting the minds and ruining the souls of the people, leading them into folly and stumbling. . . . They made the people break and burn their pipes and fiddles. If there was a foolish man here or there who demurred, the good ministers and the good elders themselves broke and burnt their instruments, saying, "Better is the small fire that warms on the little day of peace, than the great fire that burns on the great day of wrath." The people have forsaken their follies and their Sabbath-breaking, and there is no pipe, no fiddle here now.*[18]

The same islander went on to explain to Carmichael that men and women were now kept apart at the wedding feasts, the women on the one side and the men on the other. Unmarried girls were not even allowed to be seen at the feast for "fear of their life," she said, lest they be reported to the minister, who would denounce them publicly on Sunday from the pulpit.

But when Carmichael proceeded to ask if they were still allowed alcohol at the wedding feasts, the woman replied, "Oh yes, the minister is not so hard as that upon them at all." In other words, dance was denied, along with the natural intermingling of men and women in festivity, but drink was allowed. Increasingly the abuse of alcohol began to dominate the culture of the islands. A people's soul was being numbed.

Suppression of the ancient ways became persecution of Gaelic culture in the widest sense, including the forbidding of its music, language, and poetry. An old woman from Islay remembered how she and others had been treated at school when they were girls. The schoolmaster "denounced" Gaelic speech and song, she said. On getting out of school one day, they had begun to sing an old Gaelic song on their way home. "The schoolmaster heard us, however," she said, "and called us back. He punished us till the blood trickled from our fingers, although we were big girls, with the dawn of womanhood upon us. The thought of that scene fills me with indignation."[19]

Though Calvinism had tried to suppress the heart of Celtic vision and song, the greatest blow came with the Highland Clearances, the eviction of tenants from ancestral lands beginning late in the eighteenth century and growing to full force in the first half of the nineteenth. People were evicted, families and clans torn apart. The formal religion of the land did nothing to oppose this injustice, because it saw its function not as challenging the holders of political power but as sanctioning their status as ordained by God, the way religion has often been used to bless the status quo rather than to prophetically confront the abuse of power.

The basic societal structure of the Highlands and islands of Scotland had been the clan system, led by clan chiefs. The chiefs saw that members of their clan and lands were protected in exchange for service, rent, and, if required, military service. In the eighteenth century, however, the sons of clan leaders had increasingly been forced by British law to be educated in the non-Gaelic-speaking regions of the Scottish Lowlands and England. This was an attempt by the British government to exert greater control over the Celtic Highlanders.

It had the effect of weakening the clan system, separating leadership from the people. When descendants of the clan chiefs inherited the land, they increasingly saw themselves primarily as landlords rather than as leaders of their people. Living far from their own clans, in centers of power like Edinburgh and London, they began to prioritize profit over relationship and forget their sacred responsibility for the people's well-being.

In Scotland 1792 was known as the Year of the Sheep. The great landowners had realized that more money was to be made through the wool industry than through the collection of small-scale tenant-farming rents. Crofters and their families were driven off the land to the cities of Scotland or into exile across the seas. In their stead, at significantly higher rates, great swaths of land were now let to Lowland sheep farmers. The inheritance rights of Gaelic clan law were being violated. The people were torn from their ancestral land, and in their place tens of thousands of sheep were introduced.

In London, Parliament passed measures in support of the Clearances called the Land Improvements Act. In England and in the Scottish Lowlands, proponents of the new legislation even argued that the Celts were "less hardworking" and "ethnologically inferior" to Anglo-Saxons.[20] Thus, replacing them with Lowland sheep farmers was for the betterment of the Highlands and islands, they claimed. To the shame of Christianity, ministers of the Church of Scotland preached obedience to the state rather than compassion for the people. Their addiction to power and privilege had led them to forget the sacred calling of justice.

The Clearances, however, met with many acts of resistance on the ground. Eviction notices were destroyed, and many families refused to abandon their crofts. Women especially resisted the law, determined not to leave their family homesteads. Sometimes the army had to be called in to evict them by force, using violence even against the women. As Mary MacPherson, a midwife of Portree, later remembered especially for her poetry of resistance, wrote, "Their skulls were broken on the braes of Beinn Li."[21]

At times the resistance was so fierce that the army resorted to burning the houses, sometimes with whole families still in them. The thatch and roof timbers would be set on fire not only to drive out the crofters, but to prevent them from reoccupying their houses. Such was the extent of violent eviction by fire that 1819 came to be known as the Year of the Burnings. Donald MacLeod, of Sutherland, remembered that from a hill in his district on one night alone in 1819 he counted over 250 houses ablaze.

Forced to leave their land and often even their country, in what was euphemistically termed "assisted passage," families and clans were scattered. Many of the old, too frail to undertake the long journey into exile, simply became homeless, wandering the countryside, begging. Carmichael spoke to one such woman, Catherine Macphee, of Uist. She spoke of what she had witnessed in her life:

Many a thing I have seen in my own day and generation. Many a thing, O Mary, Mother of the black sorrow! I have seen the townships swept, and the big holdings being made of them, the people being driven out of the countryside to the streets of Glasgow and to the wilds of Canada, such of them as did not die of hunger and plague and smallpox while going across the ocean. I have seen the women putting the children in the carts which were being sent from Benbecula . . . to Loch Boisdale, while their husbands lay bound in the pen and were weeping beside them, without power to give them a helping hand, though the women themselves were crying aloud and their little children wailing like to break their hearts. I have seen the big strong men, the champions of the countryside, the stalwarts of the world, being bound on Loch Boisdale quay and cast into the ship as would be done

to a batch of horses or cattle in the boat, the bailiffs and the
ground-officers and the constables and the policemen gath-
ered behind them in pursuit of them. The God of life and He
only knows all the loathsome work of men on that day.[22]

The ancient prayers of protection that had been passed down
in the Hebrides for hundreds of years sounded again in the hearts
of the people:

I am placing my soul and my body
Under thy guarding this night, O Mary,
O tender Mother of the Christ of the poor,
O tender Mother of the Christ of tears.

I am placing my soul and my body
Under thy guarding this night, O Christ,
O thou son of the tears, of the wounds, of the piercings.

May the moon of moons
Be coming through thick clouds
On me and on everyone
Coming through dark tears.[23]

The people had been torn from their ancestral land and separated from each other. As Mary MacPherson, known also as
Mairi Mhor Nan Oran (Great Mary of the Songs), said in one of

her poems, "Every single thing that was of value, they plundered it from us by the law of the land."[24] Political and legal power was used as the means to an unjust end, neglecting the sacredness of the people in the name of economic gain.

Although we have no exact figures, in that accurate records were not kept, it is estimated that approximately 150,000 people were cleared. This represents half of the population of the Highlands and islands during the years of the Clearances. It is thought that about 70,000 of these were forced into emigration.

The displacement from land and community was an attack on the very soul of the people. Peggy MacCormack, of Uist, in conversation with Carmichael, lamented the changes that had been forced upon them in her lifetime:

The people were strong, healthy, and happy [in the time before the Clearances] and enjoyed life to the full in their simple homely ways. They had sheep and cattle, corn, potatoes, and poultry, milk, cheese, butter and fish, all in sufficiency. They were good to the poor, kind to the stranger, and helpful to one another. . . . There were pipers and fiddlers in almost every house, and the people sang and danced in summer time on the green grass without, and in winter time on the clay floor within. How we enjoyed ourselves in those faraway days—the old as much as the young. I often saw three and sometimes four generations dancing together on the

green grass in the golden summer sunset. Men and women
of fourscore or more—for they lived long in those days—
dancing with boys and girls of five on the green grass. Those
were the happy days and the happy nights. . . . The thought
of those young days makes my old heart both glad and sad
even at this distance of time. But the clearance came upon
us, destroying all, turning our small crofts into big farms for
the stranger, and turning our joy into misery, our gladness
into bitterness, our blessing into blasphemy, and our Chris-
tianity into mockery. O dear man, the tears come on my eyes
when I think of all we suffered and of the sorrows.[25]

This story of both the beauty and the sufferings of the people of
the western islands of Scotland is in fact a universal story. It is the
story of what has happened to native peoples and marginalized
cultures throughout the world again and again. It is a story that is
important to tell again not only because it can reawaken us to look
for the sacred in the native and the natural, but also because it can
help sharpen our awareness of the ways in which such sacredness
is tragically being violated in our world today. It is a story too that
stirs our memory of the lost native and indigenous wisdoms of the
earth and the human soul that we so desperately need at this moment in time if we are to find the way forward in our relationship
with the earth and one another.

It is important to tell also what happened to the people of the Highlands and islands after the wrongs they suffered. Some, as we have heard, were broken by the experience, crushed in body and spirit. Others undertook long journeys into foreign exile, sometimes tragically perpetrating the same wrongs that had been done to them on the native peoples of the Americas and Australia, a cycle of oppression that has repeated itself again and again in history. But there were others also who were able to access the soul force of their inheritance and act with dignity and compassion in their search for new beginnings.

Deep in this wisdom tradition is the belief that just as new life rises from the earth every spring, so new vision is forever trying to come forth from the human soul. Anything that is of God, even though pushed to the ground, will come forth again. Anything that is true, anything born of love and compassion, anything filled with true vision for justice will rise again. As Mary MacPherson, the poet of the Clearances, said, "Truth will triumph, despite the ingenuity of the wicked."[26]

There was treasure in this ancient spiritual tradition. History may say it was undone, but its way of seeing is rising afresh among us in our awareness of the earth and the creatures, in our recovered sense of the native and the natural, in our growing consciousness of life's essential oneness. It is a treasure that can serve our loving of one another and the planet. It is a treasure that can help us remember that everything born from the womb of the earth is sacred. It is a treasure that, thought to be lost, is being found again.

The people of the *Carmina Gadelica* are icons for us today of the power of poetry and song to keep alive a vision of the sacredness of the earth and every human being. For hundreds of years in the western islands of Scotland it was song that helped the people remember that the physical and the spiritual are interwoven. It was song that was used in the cycle of the seasons and in the journey of human life to keep them connected to the heart of their being, made of God. And it was song that sustained them in their times of loss, suffering, and exile.

For the people of the Hebrides this was passed down in oral form. The songs, prayers, and poems were intoned by one generation to the next over many centuries. Most of us today, however, do not belong to an oral tradition. We depend instead on the written word of our literary culture and the world of online communications and recordings. So perhaps for us today, it is a matter of accessing written prayers, printed poetry, and recorded music to help awaken us on a daily basis to the sacred within and around us.

Although we have lost much of the richness of oral tradition, we can still learn from its beauty and simplicity of practice. There is much to be said for committing a prayer to memory, for instance, or allowing a few simple words of awareness to become a personal mantra that can be repeated every day at the rising of the sun or its setting, at the beginning of a meal or the commencement of work.

When words are internalized this way, they can come forth naturally and often more deeply from within.

Although it is important to fashion new songs of the soul
for this moment in time and to be finding fresh expressions of
meditative awareness for today, there are also some beautiful utterances from the past that we can weave into our lives now. One
of the prayers from the western islands of Scotland that many
people have committed to memory is a blessing for peace. It invokes the graces of earth, air, fire, and water, and weaves these
into its devotion to Christ:

> *Deep peace of the running wave to you,*
> *Deep peace of the flowing air to you,*
> *Deep peace of the quiet earth to you,*
> *Deep peace of the shining stars to you,*
> *Deep peace of the Son of Peace to you.*[27]

Before concluding this chapter, I invite you to take a few
minutes to pay attention to what the stories and prayers of the
Carmina Gadelica have awakened in you. As you do the reflection practice below, sitting in silence, name in gratitude what has
been stirring within you from this chapter. (All of the meditative
practices are collected in the appendix, which can be used on a
daily basis to remain alert to what has been calling your inner
attention as you read this book.)

Reflection: Sacred Song

Words of Awareness

The people of the *Carmina Gadelica* carried within themselves a song of the earth and the human soul. It is a song of strength and vision that we can choose to sing in new ways today.

(Reflect for a brief time on the ways this wisdom applies to your life.)

Prayer of Awareness

Awake, O my soul,
To the ever new song of the earth that is within you.
Awake to its rhythms and seasons,
Its memories of joy and lament
And its eternal hopes of fresh buddings and births.
Awake, O my soul,
To the ever new song of the earth that is within you.

(Listen silently for a few minutes within the sacredness of your being.)

Awake, O my soul. Awake.

5

SACRED IMAGINATION: ALEXANDER JOHN SCOTT

In the Celtic world the imagination is a faculty of knowing. It is a way of remembering what we have forgotten, that spirit and matter are interwoven and that time and eternity are intermingled. The imagination is also a bridge into the future, forever opening us to ways of seeing and living that we have not yet experienced. To be made of God is to be made of sacred imagination. It is to have the capacity to dream our way into new beginnings, in our lives and in our world. Alexander John Scott helps awaken us to these possibilities.

On May 27, 1831, a young minister of the Church of Scotland stood before the nation's highest ecclesiastical court accused of heresy. He had refused to sign the Westminster Confession of Faith, the church's principal statement of belief. His name was Alexander John Scott (1805–66). Among other things, the Westminster Confession of Faith states that we are born "wholly defiled" in body and in soul, "and wholly inclined to all evil."[1]

Scott had been teaching that at the heart of Christian wisdom is the belief that the divine and the human are one. "What is most human," he said, is "the most divine: what is most divine, the most human."[2] We know this, he contended, in the tenderness and passion of human love and affection. We experience it when we weep over the sufferings of the innocent and in our indignation at injustice and wrong. All of these are deeply human and at the same time "full of divinity."[3] The infinite, he said, is "consubstantiated" with the human.[4]

Scott used the image of royal garments woven through with a golden thread to speak of the relationship between the divine and the human within us. In nineteenth-century Britain, royal state attire was still threaded with a filament of gold. If the golden thread were taken out of the garment, the whole garment would unravel. So it is, said Scott, with the interweaving of the divine in the human. If somehow it were taken out of us, we would cease to exist.

When, in his earliest teachings Scott insisted that the divine and the human are inextricably woven together, he spoke of Jesus as embodying this truth. What we see in Jesus, he said, is the divine not merely present alongside the human but "in the human."[5] And Jesus excels us not by being something other than human or more than human. He excels us, said Scott, by being truly human. He reveals the conjoining of the divine and the human that forms the essence of our being.

In keeping with these views, Scott opposed the doctrine of original sin in the Westminster Confession of Faith, which defined human nature as essentially sinful. Using the analogy of a plant suffering from blight to speak of the way sin affects our nature, he said that botanists would not define such a plant in terms of its blight, even if they had never seen that particular species of plant before. Rather, they would say that the blight is foreign to the plant, attacking its essence. So it is, said Scott, with sin's infection in our lives. It does not define our nature; it infects our nature.

The Church of Scotland felt threatened by this young teacher, aged only twenty-six. The religious press attacked him unsparingly, saying that he and his friends had enough heresy among them "to sink in time any orthodox church in Christendom."[6] In a sense, they were right! To the extent that the theology of the Church of Scotland had been built on the doctrine of original sin, Scott's vision of the oneness of the divine and the human threatened to undermine the theological foundations of the national church's teachings.

No ecclesiastical doors were opening to Scott in his own nation. So he headed south to England to a congregation in Woolwich that, although affiliated with the Scottish church, had called him to be their minister. In order to be ordained to the post, however, Scott was required by the London Presbytery of the Church of Scotland to sign the Westminster Confession of Faith as a statement of his own belief. This he simply could not and would not do. Consequently in 1831 the presbytery accused him of heresy, sending the matter up for final judgment to the General Assembly of the Church of Scotland in Edinburgh. There was little support for Scott in his homeland. In London, however, during the week leading up to his trial, nearly one thousand people met every morning at 6:30 a.m. to pray for Scott and the coming deliberations of the General Assembly.

His heresy trial began late on the evening of May 27, 1831, and proceeded through the night. During his defense Scott was constantly interrupted and accused of "insulting" the dignity of the assembly, because he had challenged the church's statement of faith. In the end Scott chose to be silent. Speaker after speaker rose to denounce him for what they called his "novelties and imaginations."[7] It was thought that nothing new could be uttered in matters of faith. Everything of ultimate value, it was assumed, had already been stated. Truth was not a living well to be accessed ever anew. It was a fixed, final, and authoritative decree issued by the church. Scott later said of his trial before the General Assembly, "not one voice had a word for me."[8]

His sentence was pronounced just before dawn. Unanimously he was found guilty of heresy, 125 votes against him, not one in his favor. He was deposed from the ministry of the Church of Scotland and banned from every pulpit in the land. But, as Scott later recounted, in remembering his walk home through Edinburgh's

New Town in the light of early dawn that day, "I was relieved, indeed, after years of inner struggle." Despite the pain of the overwhelming judgment against him, he knew a sense of deep relief within himself. He had spoken truthfully and candidly in his trial. The agonizing dispute with the church of his inheritance was finally over.

Scott returned south to England immediately, and in the months after the General Assembly his health gave way. Here was a young man who had been unanimously denounced by his own tradition. Even his father, a senior minister in the Church of Scotland, supported the decision of the assembly. Scott had been judged by both his family of birth and his family of baptism. The rejection broke him physically and emotionally. He collapsed, weakened and exhausted.

Where do we find the strength to spiritually resist what is false? This is an important question for many of us today in our struggle against systems and powers that deny the sacredness of the earth and the dignity of every human being. We need one another in this great work, like-minded souls with whom we can work, and, as we have noted in previous chapters, we also need a sense of inner authority to challenge outward power structures and well-established systems of thought. This is not work in which we can always expect to have the approval and support of the majority. Like Alexander Scott, we will sometimes feel like lone voices. Nor can we be sure that our work will ever succeed in bringing about the changes we hope for. The work must rest primarily on the integrity of the vision as well as the certainty that what we are calling for is a truth that belongs to the human soul, not just our soul. We are to help awaken it in one another and be true to it in ourselves.

After Scott regained his strength, he began to teach publicly in London. Many of those who gathered around him now were already in exile from their faith traditions, a prophetic anticipation of the vast diaspora of men and women today who, although born into the Christian tradition, no longer identify with its formal beliefs and practices. Those who sought out Scott, like the many who are in exile today, were longing for a vision that could nurture their sense of the sacredness of the earth and the human soul. Freed now from the tight constraints of Scottish Calvinism, Scott began to draw in his teachings from the Bhagavad Gita, the Quran, and the sacred scriptures of other traditions.

Scott was a broad soul and a brilliant mind, with wide-ranging intellectual interests; he read original texts in Latin, Greek, Hebrew, and Anglo-Saxon and mastered the modern languages of French, German, and Italian. His brilliance, as is often the case with inspiring minds, was coupled with eccentricity. A delightful story about him tells of how he failed to turn up for a Sunday lecture he was supposed to be giving in

London on one occasion. His friends, still concerned about his health, rushed to Scott's house, only to find him sitting on the study floor surrounded by piles of books. He had forgotten it was Sunday!

Earlier, his teachings had focused primarily on the sacredness of the human soul, but now in London Scott began to articulate a second major feature of Celtic wisdom, the sacredness of the earth. It is, he said, "a transparency" through which the Light of God can be seen.[10] Like the succession of great Celtic teachers before him over the centuries, he pointed to the Light within all light, the Soul behind all souls, the Life at the heart of all life:

> *Who can gaze upon the moon beams stealing through the boughs of the dark forest trees—or the fir [tree] glowing in relief against the clear amber sky, or the mountain scenery which seems to partake more of the sky above it than of the soft verdure that reposes at its feet—without feeling that they all speak of this world transformed and glorified, and of the world above made ours.[11]*

Drawing on the teachings of the ninth-century Irish scholar John Scotus Eriugena, Scott said everything is essentially a theophany, a "manifestation" of God, a showing of the divine.[12]

Like Eriugena, he refers to the two books through which God is speaking, the sacred text of scripture, physically small, and the "grand volume of God's utterance," the universe.[13] A person with the Bible in one hand, he said, is not released from the study of God in that other book, the sacred text of the earth and of everything that has being. We need both.

The awareness of the sacred that we access in nature is not a doctrinal or propositional knowing, said Scott. It belongs "to some deeper part of the human being."[14] It is the way lovers know each other, with their whole beings, heart and mind, body and soul, knowing the spiritual in the physical. "Forms, colors, motions, sounds"—it is through these that we encounter the presence of the divine, says Scott. "This is the value of the sun, moon and stars, of earth and sea, of trees and flowers, of the bodies of men and women, the looks of human countenances, the tones of human voices."[15] It is through these that the divine is made known to us.

A later disciple of Scott's, James Picton, said that Scott taught him to see "the fathomless mystery involved in the mere existence of a pebble."[16] In a book he later wrote entitled *The Mystery of Matter*, Picton described this vision of reality as an expression of "Christian pantheism."[17] He used this term in an attempt to hold together his love of Christ and his love of the earth, and the sense of spirit and matter inseparably intermingled.

But the term *pantheism* did not accurately describe Picton's vision, for it literally means "everything is God." It is derived from the Greek words *pan* (meaning "all things") and *theos* ("God"). But this is not in fact what Picton was teaching, nor is this what Scott had taught him. The problem was that Picton did not yet have access to the later and much more accurate term *panentheism*, a word that was not coined until the end of the nineteenth century. It means "God is in all things." So not just *pan* and *theos*, all things are God, but the critically important addition of the Greek word *en* (meaning "in"). God is *in* all things. This was the vision that Picton had received from Scott, the sense of spirit shining through matter, the transcendent and the immanent inseparably interwoven, the Life within all life.

Scott's panentheistic vision anticipated what is perhaps the greatest prophetic challenge facing Christianity today. Will we continue in our language and expressions of faith to give the impression that the light of Christ is somehow essentially alien to the matter of the universe and to what is deepest in every human being? Or will we be guided in our love of the light that is in Christ to look for this light, adore it, and serve it deep within the mystery of one another and the body of the earth?

This, I believe, is the most pressing issue facing the Church today. The extent to which we faithfully address this issue will be the extent to which we either serve the world's well-being, by helping reawaken it to a sense of the sacred in all things, or continue to be irrelevant to the world's well-being, by inferring that sacredness is somehow the property only of certain people and certain places rather than the birthright and essence of all.

By the early 1840s Scott was moving among some of the most creative thinkers of nineteenth-century Britain, writers like the philosopher Thomas Carlyle, the artist and social thinker John Ruskin, and the naturalist and geologist Charles Darwin. Scott believed that we are to listen to the insights of every discipline of thought. "There is a harmony in all truth," he said, "a mutual dependence. All its lines converge . . . [and whoever] will try to do without any of them will find that the rest must suffer."[18] In other words, if we ignore the insights of ecology, for instance, then our spirituality will be less profound, our psychology will be lacking, and our economics and politics will be misdirected. "To truly understand," said Scott, "is to find a unity."[19]

By the middle of the nineteenth century a conflict was looming between religion and science in relation to Darwin's evolutionary theories in Britain. Scott, however, taught that it is a false religion that is contrary to true science, and it is a false science that ignores the great insights of spiritual wisdom. The spiritual and the physical utterances of God are one.

As Darwin was advancing his theory of evolution, Scott at the same time was developing his awareness of the interrelationship of all things, the organic unity of the earth. Julia Wedgwood, the niece of Charles Darwin, later said that Scott was "the first to re-flect this dawning truth, even now only just above our horizon."[20] It is "the most inward of all unity," said Scott, "the unity that works outwardly into all the various manifestations of the visible creation; the unity that is not a unity at the branches . . . but a unity at the root."[21] For Scott this was the unity of the divine deep within the multiplicity of the universe, what he called "the Being on which all being rests."[22]

Given his belief in the sacred interrelationship of all things, Scott defined sin as being out of harmony with what is deepest in the earth and in one another. Heaven and hell, he said, are present realities. It is when we are true to the sacred interrelationship of earth and humanity that we experience heaven within us and between us. It is when we are unfaithful to this interrelationship that we create hell on earth for one another and the creatures. Redemption, therefore, is about overcoming disunity. It is about the essential oneness deep in all things finding faithful expression in our lives and world, including our relationship with the earth. Redemption happens when we wake up to this sacred interrelationship of all things and translate it into action.

By the late 1840s Scott was attracting younger disciples to his teachings. It was both the breadth of his vision and, as one of his students put it, the "simplicity" of his Christianity that drew them.[23] In this too Scott was anticipating the spiritual quest of many today, the desire to access the powerful simplicity of Jesus's wisdom

without having to consent to Christianity's convoluted propositional statements *about* Jesus. Scott's emphasis was on *knowing* the
sacred rather than knowing *about* the sacred. It was about experiencing the divine with our whole being rather than just assenting
to doctrinal belief with our minds. The type of knowing that Scott
modeled for his students was what he called "the heart in the head,
the head in the heart, the equipoise of the soul," a balance of mind
and heart, an integration of reason and intuition.[24]

Scott welcomed this younger generation of followers, and allowed them to come close to him personally. As one of his students
said, he "was as natural, and simple, and gentle as a child, and as
easily amused."[25] The same young man proceeded to describe going
to the theater with Scott one evening and having to take him
out halfway through the performance because he was laughing
uncontrollably. Scott's mature learning and wisdom were colorfully combined with an innocence and childlike playfulness in
his character. And it was the childlikeness of his imagination that
increasingly came to the fore in his teachings.

One of the young students to be attracted to Scott during
these years was the author, poet, and clergyman George Mac-
Donald (1824–1905), who later became the nineteenth-century
equivalent of J. K. Rowling in British literature. At this stage,
however, MacDonald was studying theology at Highbury College in London. The Principal of the College did not approve of
Scott's teachings, so MacDonald and some of his fellow students

would sneak out in the evenings to hear Scott teach publicly. What particularly captivated the young MacDonald was the "boldness" of Scott's imagination.[26] Through Scott he came to see that the imagination is like a key to bringing all things back into relationship again, reimagining our way into the essential interconnectedness of the universe.

In time MacDonald was *also* accused of heresy. He too was defrocked, in his case from the ministry of the Congregational Church in England. During this critical time in MacDonald's life he sought sanctuary with Scott, even residing for some months in the Scott household. This is when he began to write, transposing Scott's spiritual vision into literary works of the imagination, one of the most famous of which is his fairy tale *The Princess and the Goblin*.

The Princess and the Goblin is the story of a young princess named Irene. Her father was king of a great country comprised of many mountains and valleys. She resided in a castle on the side of one of the mountains, halfway between its summit and the valley below. There she lived at peace, in harmony with both the villagers and the creatures and plants of the mountains.

But within the mountain there were hollow places, huge caverns and subterranean rivers. Living in these dark hidden chambers were strange creatures called goblins. Legend had it that at one stage they had lived above ground as human beings, but they had become selfish and unnatural, choosing instead to live away from the sun below ground in the dark and damp.

The goblins were not merely ugly; they were grotesque, "subnatural," writes MacDonald. They had two evil projects underway. The first was the burrowing of a tunnel into the foundations of the castle to kidnap the princess. The second was the plan to divert the mountain's mightiest subterranean river into the shafts of the king's copper mines to drown the workers and to sabotage the kingdom's source of revenue.

The princess and her household knew nothing of these plans. But around the time of their inception Irene discovered in the castle a curious old winding staircase covered in layers of dust. She followed it up and up into the tower until she came to a turret room at the very top. There she found a beautiful old woman sitting at a spinning wheel. Her face was smooth with the beauty of youth, but her eyes glistened with the wisdom of the ages. She said to Irene, "Come in, my dear. You are welcome here."

In her beautiful dome-shaped turret room, the old woman explained to Irene that she was her great-great-grandmother, although MacDonald adds that she was in fact the beautiful mother of all grandmothers, and that the thread she was spinning was a golden thread that was woven through all things. Sometimes the thread could be glimpsed glistening in the moonlight, but usually it could not be seen with the human eye, only felt. If ever Irene was in danger, said the woman, she was simply to feel for the thread with her finger and follow wherever it led. It might take her through strange and frightening places, but in the end it would lead her safely back to the grandmother.

Some months later Irene was awakened in the night by the sound of rumbling deep in the foundations of the castle. Frightened, she felt for the thread and found it. However, it led her not to the winding staircase, but instead out into the darkness of the night, which she had been warned never to venture into alone for fear of the goblins. The thread led her up and up the mountainside until it came to the simplest of cottages in which a humble family lived. There she was welcomed and given shelter for the night.

Meanwhile the goblins had broken into the wine cellar of the castle in their plans to seize the princess. At the same time, they had set in motion their second scheme, flooding the king's mines. But the goblins had miscalculated and, instead of releasing a torrent of subterranean water into the mine, they flooded the tunnel they were using to break into the castle. So the goblins were caught in their own scheme of destruction, and their drowned bodies washed up into the basement of the castle.

The princess was safe. All was well with the inhabitants of the valley. Peace had come again to the kingdom.

Although fairy tales are written more for the imagination than for analysis, we can discern four main themes in the story.

First, the Sacred Presence is close to us, within the very household of our being, like the grandmother in the attic. The sacredness of this presence is woven like a golden thread through all things.

Second, we are of the divine. Like great-grandchildren of the Sacred Feminine, we are born to live in relationship, in peace (which is the meaning of the name Irene) with one another and the earth. Third, although we are of the divine, we are capable of terrible falseness, or what MacDonald calls the "subnatural." And this subnaturalness in us, as is the case with the goblins in the story, can threaten the foundations of our being.

And, finally, despite our capacity for falseness, the golden thread is not severed. Evil can cause horrible suffering, but its very nature is self-destructive. Deep within us is the gift of our sacred lineage—if we are true to it, we will be led to new beginnings.

Years ago, I was telling this fairy tale at a retreat center in Pennsylvania in the Blue Ridge Mountains. In the front row was a woman in her eighties. I noticed as I began to tell the story that there were tears in her eyes. At the end of the evening she spoke to me about why she had been so moved. When she was a little girl, maybe seventy-five years earlier, her grandmother had often read this story to her. But the grandmother had died when she was still a young girl, and she had never heard the fairy tale again. In fact, she had come to wonder if the story really existed or if she had just imagined it.

In a sense we are all being invited to remember what at some level we knew in the innocence of our childhood, but have since forgotten or come to doubt, that light is woven through all things like a thread of gold.

In the literary genres of both fairy tales and novels, MacDonald communicated Scott's vision to hundreds of thousands of readers. His works later influenced some of the greatest modern authors of imaginative works, like J. R. R. Tolkien, who wrote the *Lord of the Rings* series, and C. S. Lewis, who wrote *The Chronicles of Narnia*. Lewis spoke of MacDonald's writings as having baptized his imagination. He saw that the world of the imaginal is not simply fantasy, that it can be a pathway into deeper knowing.

Scott attracted around him not just young writers and theologians of the day but also some of the greatest literary and artistic figures of mid-nineteenth-century Britain. At his weekly soirées at Gloucester Crescent in London on Wednesday evenings, Scott would open his house to artists and thinkers from many disciplines. One could find there Charles Dickens or William Thackeray, Thomas Carlyle or John Ruskin, Lady Byron or, when he was in town, Frédéric Chopin. These were gatherings that nurtured creativity and imaginary vision.

In 1848 Scott was appointed professor of English literature

at University College London, the only seat of higher education in the country that was free from religious tests. All other universities in England at this time awarded degrees only to those who were willing to sign the Thirty-Nine Articles, the Church of England's statement of faith. Scottish universities had the same requirement in relation to the Westminster Confession of Faith.

It was at University College London that Scott now further developed his understanding of the imagination, especially in relation to poetry, although he touched on the role of the imagination in every field of knowledge from science and literature to theology. True poetic speech, he said, is the imagination accessing the poetry of the universe itself and reflecting it in spoken and written form. All things are fashioned by the great imaginer. To be made of God, therefore, is to be made of sacred imagination. It is through this sacred faculty of knowing that we can access more deeply the very heart of reality. The imagination is the creative "dance of the mind" reflecting the interrelationship of all things.[27]

Scott gave many years of his life to the highest forms of study, including helping to establish the first institution of higher education for women in Britain free of religious tests, Bedford College in London, and he was passionate about grounding his vision in the work of justice. The mid-nineteenth century in Europe was a time of political struggle and revolution. The French socialist revolution in 1848 reverberated throughout the whole of Europe, giving rise also to social and political unrest in Britain. Scott was alert to this turmoil throughout Europe and was close to the exiled leaders of the Italian revolutionary movement for democracy.

He had been critical of the way organized religion either ignored justice issues or was used to sanction the political status quo and the inequities of British society. How did religion ever come to be "another name for self-interest," he asked, "or at best for its extension into eternity," in which the devout are more concerned about the salvation of their own souls than the well-being of humanity?[28] And to those who used religion to justify the existing political order, Scott said, "God is the God of order, but not necessarily pledged to that particular form of order by which your quiet and your wealth seem to you to be best secured. God will not be taken into your pay; God will not submit to act as a preventive police for you."[29] The divine, he said, is not on the side of privilege; it is on the side of justice.

After the socialist victory in Paris in 1848, riots followed almost immediately in the United Kingdom. On April 10 of that year, tens of thousands marched on London with a national petition demanding reform. Many feared this was the starting signal for violent revolution in Britain. The next day Scott met with some of his closest friends, including Frederick Denison Maurice and Charles Kingsley. This was the beginning of a movement that came to be known as Christian socialism. It was the first attempt in Europe to bring socialist principles into relationship with Christian vision. The Christian socialists began a weekly periodical called *Politics for the People*, which in its first issue the following month said, "Liberty, Fraternity, and Unity . . . are intended for every people under heaven."[30] Weekly meetings with workers were organized, and the first Workers Cooperative was established. Scott and his circle played a significant role in the peaceful and gradual recognition of socialism in Britain.

In 1854 Scott also helped establish the first Working Men's College in Britain. The extension of higher education to the working classes, said Scott, was preparing for the most beneficial and the most radical of revolutions. During these years Scott more fully developed his threefold vision of higher education. First, through the training of the mind, education would enable people to acquire a greater "consciousness of soul" and thereby become more aware of what is true in the universe and in humanity.

Second, it would nurture a greater "strength of soul," by encouraging individuals to be guided with moral integrity in their lives by the interrelationship of all things. Third, it would foster a greater "beauty of soul," by which Scott meant learning to love the universe and care for others as one cares for oneself, even at the cost of sacrifice. Consciousness of soul, strength of soul, beauty of soul—this was the "revolution," he said, that higher education could be part of.[31]

This is the revolution that is needed in our world today if we are to truly wake up to the sacredness of the earth and every human being and do what we can to serve this sacredness in one another and the creatures. Again, we need consciousness of soul, a waking up to the sacred interrelationship of all things, of every species and life-form, race and nation. We again need strength of soul, a commitment to live in accordance with this interrelationship, both individually and collectively. We again need beauty of soul, the willingness to serve this oneness with love, even at the cost of sacrifice. This combination of conscious awareness, inner strength, and commitment to love is capable of bringing about radical change in our lives and world.

After more than a decade of activity in the field of education and social reform, including helping to establish the beginnings of Manchester University as the second major institution of higher education in Britain free from religious tests, Scott's health failed him. In November 1865 he headed for Veytaux in Switzerland in the hope that the natural hot springs of Lake Geneva would revive him. But it was too late. On January 12, 1866, Scott died at the age of sixty.

At his funeral in the cemetery of Clarens on the shores of Lake Geneva, when the words "I am the resurrection and the life" (John 11:25) were spoken, a shaft of sunlight burst through the dark clouds that had formed overhead. For the small company of family and friends who gathered at the grave this was like a reassurance of what Scott had always taught, that darkness will not prevail against the light.

After his death he was spoken of in Britain as one of the master teachers of the age and as the prophet of "an awakening soul."[32] Scott's vision was well ahead of its time, anticipating some of the most important modern precepts of life's essential interrelatedness. But he was not a writer, so his voice faded with the passing of the generation of those he had inspired in his own lifetime. First and foremost, he was a teacher whose imagination and poetic speech had awakened the souls of his listeners.

Scott left no major corpus of writings, so much so that, when I was a young PhD student at the University of Edinburgh in the late 1970s and proposed doing my doctoral research on Alexander John Scott, I was told there was likely not enough source material upon which to base my research. But a generous professor, Alec Cheyne, believed in me enough to give me a year to prove to his satisfaction that there was sufficient original material available. This I discovered primarily in newspaper accounts of Scott's public addresses and in the many personal letters of correspondence between Scott and leading thinkers of the time, archives of which have been preserved in libraries and universities throughout Britain.

By the end of my three years of research I had spent so much time with Scott that I was having frequent conversations with him in my dreams at night. As a prophet of the imagination, he would likely have approved! In the years since then I would say that I have never delivered a talk nor written a single page for publication that does not in some way reflect the abiding influence of this great Celtic teacher on my life.

"The sum of the whole matter is this," he said, that the most important work for us to do "from year to year, from month to month, from hour to hour is to combine earth and heaven, time and eternity."[33] This is the role of the sacred imagination, to help us remember the "curve of oneness" from which we have come. It will strengthen us in the sacred work of seeking true relationship with one another and the earth.

Scott is an icon for us of the imaginal mind. He saw that the imagination reflects the very nature of the universe, which interweaves countless strands of life into a single fabric of reality. He also saw that the imagination could play a key role in dreaming the way forward in our lives and world, reweaving into new patterns of relationship what has been torn apart.

We are broken in so many ways, both within ourselves personally and between us as nations, races, and religions. If we are to be part of reweaving the fabric of life, both individually and collectively, we urgently need to access the imagination again. We have the capacity, pure gift of God within us, to imagine ways of living and relating that we have never experienced before. The history of the universe itself is like a dream with layer upon layer of interrelationship and strand upon strand of new beginnings. We have emerged out of this web of creative interrelationship, and we carry, even within the genetic makeup of our being, something of the memory of successive beginnings since the origins of time. We can therefore open ourselves to the possibility of new interrelationships and new beginnings that have never been before. Scott inspires us to boldly imagine, even when it might seem there is no way forward.

Before concluding this chapter, I invite you to take a few minutes to pay attention to what Scott has awakened in you. As you do the reflection practice below, sitting in silence, name in gratitude what has been stirring within you from this chapter. (All of the meditative practices are collected in the appendix, which can be used on a daily basis to remain alert to what has been calling your inner attention as you read this book.)

REFLECTION: SACRED IMAGINATION

WORDS OF AWARENESS

Alexander John Scott taught that in every moment and encounter of life we can imagine the intermingling of heaven and earth, time and eternity, spirit and matter. Together we can dream our way forward into what has never been before.

(Reflect for a brief time on the ways this wisdom applies to your life.)

PRAYER OF AWARENESS

Awake, O my soul,
To the sacred dreams that are stirring within you.
Awake to the imaginations of the heart
And the cherished hopes of what is yet to be.
Do not be afraid.
Awake, O my soul.
To the sacred dreams that are stirring within you.

(Listen silently for a few minutes within the sacredness of your being.)

Awake, O my soul. Awake.

SACRED EARTH: JOHN MUIR

In Celtic wisdom we remember the earth as sacred. Every tree and bush, every flower and creature, every hill and mountain is on fire with the divine. The life within all life is holy. What we do to the body of the earth is what we do to God.

Perhaps the greatest modern prophet of ecological consciousness and action is John Muir (1838–1914). He can be called an American Celt. Born in Dunbar, Scotland, he moved as a boy with his family to Wisconsin in 1849. In the following decades the Celtic vision of earth's sacredness found in him radical expression. Every life-form, he said, and every rock formation is "throbbing" and "pulsing" with the divine. Even the stars are being pulsed onward by "the heart of God."[1]

Where did Muir access this cherished Celtic image of listening within all things for the heartbeat of God? We do not know exactly. But we *do* know that it did not come through his father, Daniel Muir, a narrow, angry Calvinist who tried to teach the young Muir that we are "poor worms of the dust, conceived in sin."[2]

The tension we see in the Muir family was also being played out in the soul of the entire nation at this point in mid-nineteenth century Scotland. There were men and women offering their morning prayer at the rising of the sun or chanting their night prayer under the whiteness of the moon, addressing the Light within all light, the true life of every life. Arrayed against this ancient way of seeing, however, was the established religion of the land attempting to beat such practices out of the people.

Something of the Celtic strand of seeing came to Muir through his maternal grandfather, David Gilrye, who lived across the street from him in Dunbar when he was growing up. It was his grandfather who nurtured the young Muir's sense of open-eyed wonder at nature and encouraged his boyhood expeditions along the coastline. As Muir later wrote:

> When I was a boy in Scotland I was fond of everything that was wild, and all my life I've been growing fonder and fonder of wild places and wild creatures. . . . And best of all to watch the waves in awful storms thundering on the black headlands and craggy ruins of the old Dunbar Castle when the sea and the sky, the waves and the clouds, were mingled together as one.[3]

Muir was later to say, "All terrestrial things are essentially celestial"; that is, everything earthly is of heaven, all matter is essentially spirit.[4] The earth, he said, is a divine "incarnation."[5] Here, Muir uses a word that most of Western Christianity has reserved exclusively for Jesus. Muir applies it not just to Jesus, not even just to humanity and the creatures, but to the matter of the earth itself. Even earth's geological formations, he says, are "heaven incarnate"; the rocks can be called "instonations" of God.[6] Everything is in essence spirit, incarnated in flesh, in leaves, in rock. All these varied forms of matter "are simply portions of God," wrote Muir. They are all of "the God essence."[7]

What his father taught him was the Bible—apparently to the exclusion of everything else. Muir later described him as "my all-Bible father,"[8] who believed that no other book was necessary. By the age of eleven the young Muir had been forced to learn the entire New Testament as well as much of the Old Testament by heart and, as he poignantly adds, "by sore flesh."[9] In other words, he was beaten if he incorrectly recited scripture, a tragically common method of education in Calvinist Scotland, which failed to respect the inherent dignity of the child.

Muir later came to see that there is another sacred text, the universe. The winds, the waters, the springs, he says, are all "words of God."[10] The earth, Muir realized, is like a "divine manuscript."[11] And, echoing Eriugena in the ninth century, he said that there are "two books" through which God is speaking, the little book, namely, the holy book of scripture, and the big book, the cosmos.[12] The great sacred text of the universe, he said, is a living unfolding text, and God is still "writing passages" for us to learn from.[13]

Jesus's Sermon on the Mount is being preached on every mount, said Muir. Every mountain invites us to awaken to the divine. Every living thing is a disclosure of the earth's sacredness. "The beauty of its letters and sentences burn through me like fire," he said. Prophetically Muir announced that the universe is a "Bible" that will one day be read by all.[14] He anticipated the growing earth-consciousness of today, in which nearly every great discipline of thought and study is encouraging us to consult the earth as our teacher and to allow its essential interrelatedness to guide us in our vision of reality and in our living.

In 1849, when the Muir family moved from Scotland to establish a farm in Wisconsin, near the town of Portage, Muir was eleven years old. The decade that followed was filled with hard work from morning to night for Muir, including occasional beatings from his father. In his later teens, if the family was up at 5 a.m. to begin the day's work, Muir would be up at 3 a.m. to study, reading anything he could get his hands on, especially from the natural sciences.

At the age of twenty-two Muir enrolled at the University of Wisconsin in nearby Madison. There he met Ezra Carr, a professor of geology, who first introduced him to evolutionary thought. Darwin's *On the Origin of Species* had been published the previous year, in 1859. Muir now began to comprehend that everything in the universe was seeking new form, new manifestation. The earth was forever unfolding.

Equally important as the beginning of his geological studies with Ezra Carr was his introduction to the professor's wife, Jeanne Carr. Their friendship would go on to help shape the direction of his life. Although he does not call her this, she was effectively an *anamchara* to him, a role that, as we have seen, was so cherished in the Celtic world from the earliest centuries. Jeanne became the "friend" or "lover" of his soul. In years to come, primarily in correspondence from afar, he would share with her the unfolding awareness of his heart and mind in ways that helped him become more conscious of the vision that was awakening in him.

The context of his time at the University of Wisconsin was Civil War America. But to see, as he later described it, the "First Soul" deep in every soul meant he could not possibly take another's life, even in the cause of a noble ideal.[15] Given his pacifist convictions, he sought to avoid being drafted into the Union Army. So in 1864 he headed north by foot through the woods of Wisconsin and crossed into Canada. There he found sanctuary and worked at a sawmill in Meaford, Ontario.

After the war he returned to the United States, and in 1866 was employed at a wagon-wheel factory in Indianapolis. He had an inventive side that seemed to hold great promise in the field of mechanical engineering, but in 1867 he suffered an industrial accident that nearly blinded him. He spent six weeks confined to a darkened room, fearing he might never see again.

Jeanne Carr described how, when Muir began to recover his physical sight, he simultaneously began to experience a new inner way of seeing, what she called seeing with the "eye within the eye," or what in Celtic wisdom over the centuries had been called seeing with the eye of the heart.[16] He was now aware of a glory deep in all things. The earth had become for him "a burning bush," as he put it, with reference to the story from Hebrew scriptures of Moses encountering a bush that was on fire without being consumed. At the heart of the fire was the presence of the divine. Similarly, Muir now began to see a sacredness shining at the heart of all things. As he later described the glory of sunset on a mountaintop in California, "Yellow gold, the last of day, not gilding but golding to flame the tops of the trees. . . . Spiritual fire burning in every tree, in every bush, in every stone. . . . Every bush is a burning bush."[17]

What Muir is describing is essentially the child's way of seeing, an open-eyed wonder at the universe. The trauma of nearly losing his physical sight and then the gift of its restoration reconnected him to the grace of childhood's sight. He had reawakened to the earth as sacred.

With his eyes opened to the glory, Muir decided in 1867 to leave the city for what he called a "pilgrimage" into the heart of the natural world.[18] He set out on a one-thousand-mile walk to Florida on the leafiest, least-trodden path he could find. Immersed in nature, Muir now began to prophetically speak of the interrelationship of all things and the sacredness of every species.

He asked, why should humanity value itself as more than "a small part of the one great unit of creation"?[19] The universe would be incomplete without humanity, but it would also be incomplete without any one of earth's other species. More and more he came to view the creatures as "our earth-born companions," as he called them, or, using the phrase of his favorite Scottish poet, Robert Burns, our "fellow mortals."[20] The human species comes from heaven, he said, but not any more directly than daisies or bears! They all come from the "one fountain Soul."[21]

The next year, 1868, Muir sailed to California and immediately set out from San Francisco on foot for Yosemite Valley, where he spent his first summer as a shepherd. He began in the Sierra foothills and made his way up into the mountains. Entering them, he said, was like coming home:

> *Now we are fairly into the mountains, and they are into us. We are fairly living now. What bright seething white-fire enthusiasm is bred in us. . . . We are part of nature . . . [which] like a fluid seems to drench and steep us throughout, as the whole sky and the rocks and flowers are drenched with God.*[22]

If his new way seeing in Indianapolis had been like an epiphany that awakened him to the Light that is in all things, entering Yosemite was like being "born again," as he put it.[23] It was as if his true nature were coming forth anew. "Never shall I forget my baptism in this font."[24] The earth, he realized, is not simply "clothed with light, but wholly composed of it."[25] This was not just a seeing with his eyes; it was an experiencing with his whole body and soul, touching "naked God," as he said.[26]

This led him to see that walking barefoot can be a deep way of knowing. We need to know with our "heels," he said, as well as with our heads.[27] When our soles touch the earth our soul more readily awakens to the sacredness of the earth. Again, for Muir, it was like the story of the burning bush in the Hebrew scriptures in which Moses hears the words, "Remove the sandals from your feet, for the place on which you are standing is holy ground" (Exod. 3:5). A story of revelation such as this, like every great spiritual revelation, points to what is deep in every place and every moment, and the greater the revelation, the deeper it is pointing. All ground is holy. Every moment is sacred. The invitation is to wake up to this sacredness in all things.

Late in 1869 he moved to Yosemite on a more permanent basis, working in a lumber mill that processed wind-felled trees. There he built a little cabin over a stream, so that in bed at night he could hear the sound of the waters rushing beneath him. Increasingly he spoke of the wildness of God, the untamableness of the divine. During a storm one day he tied himself to the top of a one-hundred-foot Douglas fir tree, so that he could sway with the wind and hear all around him trees being uprooted by the storm and crashing to the ground.

More and more he knew himself to be part of wild nature, "kin to everything."[28] Even his appearance became wild and unkempt; he looked increasingly like a Hebrew prophet. In a letter to Jeanne Carr he described how he would spend his day off each week, Sunday, "in the spirit world," roaming from peak to peak and from meadow to meadow, shouting his praises aloud like a Methodist preacher in a revival service. "I am in the woods, woods, woods," he writes, "and they are in me-ee-ee. The King tree [sequoia] and I have sworn eternal love."[29] For Muir, opening to the sacred was about opening to the elemental. As he was later to say, "In God's wildness lies the hope of the world."[30]

If Muir is right, that our hope lies in God's wildness, his statement holds enormous implications today for the human journey and the well-being of the planet. It means at least three significant things. First, it means that our source of hope is already present, deep within the wildness of the natural world. We need to let go of our notion that what the earth primarily needs is us, our sophisticated civilization and our advanced technologies. Our role, rather, is to remember that we need the earth and the wildness that is within her. We are not called to be masters of the earth but lovers of the earth, harnessing what we have acquired in the development of our civilization and scientific knowledge to serve her, not dominate her. Part of what we owe the earth right now is the space and time she needs to heal from the damage we have inflicted on her.

The second implication of Muir's statement, that in God's wildness lies the hope of the world, is that we need to allow the wildernesses of the natural world to more fully awaken us. There is hope for the human journey to the extent that we come back into true relationship with the earth's wildness. This will affect not only what we do with our leisure time, as we realize the importance of getting back out into wilderness landscapes. It will also affect our work time, as we learn again from the rhythms and seasons of the earth rather than pretending that we can work nonstop and still be well. Similarly, we can allow the earth to remind us of what a healthy diet is and how to farm the land and harvest the seas sustainably. It will inspire our approach to the planning of our cities, the restructuring of our metropolises and neighborhoods, in ways that reflect our need of nature's wildness around us and among us.

Third, it will mean getting in touch with the wildness of the divine within ourselves. Our hope lies not primarily in human reason and scientific analysis, but in the untamed regions of intuition and human imagination within us. We come from the "one fountain Soul," as Muir said. This is not a domesticated fountain, neatly confined to the manicured gardens of civilization. It is a wildly natural source, deeper than any boundaries of our making, eternally free in its surging, inspiring us forever to be and to do what we have not yet consciously known. "We little know how much wildness there is in us," said Muir.[31]

To say that Muir knew the sacredness of the wild does not mean that he was untouched by the cultural conditioning and stereotypes of his time, in particular with regard to the way native tribes lived close to the earth. In 1869, when he was still a young man early in his time in California, he encountered Native Americans in the foothills of the Sierras. In his diary he wrote, "A strangely dirty and irregular life these dark-eyed, dark-haired, half-happy savages lead in this clean wilderness."[32]

If we are looking for a perfect prophet, if indeed there is such a thing, we should not look to the early Muir. At this stage he still carried many internal contradictions from his inherited culture and upbringing, but he did evolve. By the early 1880s, when he was in his forties, Muir was working closely with native guides in Alaska. A local chief with whom he worked spoke with deep gratitude of his encounter with Muir: "I am an old man . . . but never until now have I felt a white man's heart. All white men I have met before wanted to get something from us. But now for the first time the Indian and the white man are eye to eye, heart to heart."[33] Muir had shifted. He had more fully awakened to the sacred within every culture, every race, every nation.

The early Muir's integrity was diminished by his racial prejudices, but he was always true to the wildness of the natural within himself. During a mighty storm one evening in the mountains, he wrote from his cabin, "I feel wild and unmanageable. . . . How gloriously it storms! The pines are in ecstasy, and I feel I must go out to them . . . and mingle in the storm and make some studies."[34] Muir was drawn to the wildness of the natural, but he was also drawn to understand it. It was not just a matter of mingling with the storm. It was also about becoming more deeply aware of the earth's energies and her long story of unfolding. But always Muir's approach to study and observation was eccentric:

> This was my method of study. I drifted about from rock to rock, from stream to stream, from grove to grove. . . . When I discovered a new plant, I sat down beside it for a minute or day, to make its acquaintance and try to hear what it had to say. . . . I asked the boulders I met, whence they came from and whither they were going.[35]

Muir combined within himself a sense of the vast geological unfolding of the earth over millions of years with a depth of personal feeling for the holy particularity of every expression of life.

He tells the story of crossing a river one day and spotting a variety of orchid he had never seen before. The orchids were so beautiful and full of life, he says, that he "sat down beside them and wept for joy."[36] In Muir a reawakening to the earth was not just a scientific discipline; it was also a spiritual response. It was not just a perception of the sacred in all things; it was a relationship with the sacred in all things.

Muir's studies led him to two foundational realizations: he saw that everything is in flux and that everything is interrelated. "Everything is flowing—going somewhere," he said, "animals and so-called lifeless rocks as well as water."[37] Everything is in a single mighty current of change. Creation he saw not as an act of the past that is finished. Rather, "it is going on today as much as it ever was. But Nature," he said, "is not in a hurry."[38]

For Muir, the flow of the universe was both sacred and evolutionary. "We all flow from one fountain Soul," he said, which is "saturating all and fountainizing all."[39] The God essence flows through mountain granites as much as through trees, whether living or fallen. It even flows through death itself, he said. "These brown weeds and grasses that we say are dying in autumn frosts are in a gushing glowing current of life; they too are Godful."[40]

Muir was aware that life has flowed to us through all that has preceded humanity in the universe, through the sun, moon, and stars, through mountain ranges, plants, and animals. They are our parents, he said. "The sun shines not simply on us but in us. The rivers flow not [just] past us but through us . . . and every bird song, wind song, and storm song [is our song]."[41] To know the beauty of a mountain, for instance, is to know something of the mountain's beauty within us. We are "a bundle of world," he said.[42] We are the universe squeezed into human form.

As sons and daughters of the universe, we are being invited to remember the interrelationship of all things. All that God has made, he said, is joined and "one-d" by forces as irresistible as gravitation.[43] Every atom is married to every other atom. "When we try to pick out anything by itself," said Muir, "we find it hitched to everything else in the universe."[44] What we do to one part of life we do to the whole. Muir, like so many of the Celtic prophets before him, was announcing the growing realization of earth's interrelatedness that we are in the midst of today.

By the early 1870s the prophet Muir was beginning to attract visitors to Yosemite. Teachers, academics, and the merely curious came to see him in the mountains. Among them was the philosopher and poet Ralph Waldo Emerson (1803–82), who described Muir as the prophet of nature he had long been waiting for. Likewise, Muir loved Emerson, whom he described as the most "sequoia-like soul" he'd ever met: "His smile was as sweet and calm as morning light on mountains. . . . I felt here was a man I had been seeking . . . as sincere as the trees."[45]

There are fascinating resonances between Celtic wisdom and the American transcendentalism of thinkers like Ralph Waldo

Emerson and Henry David Thoreau. Both traditions look to the inherent sacredness of humanity and nature. Muir had found in Emerson and Thoreau kindred spirits and inspiring minds.

Early in the 1870s friends began encouraging Muir to write, both to name the sacredness of nature and to denounce the sacrilege of nature that was happening in the name of the "almighty dollar," as he later called it. Nineteenth-century America saw half of its forest cover eliminated, plus much of the wildlife that depended upon it. This was largely driven by greed, but some of it by sheer thoughtlessness. In 1854, for instance, a magnificent giant sequoia called the Mother of the Forest, over 300 feet high and 25 feet in diameter, had been stripped of its bark so that it could be shipped to London, to the Crystal Palace, for exhibition. The tree consequently died. It was later proved to be over twenty-five hundred years old. This was unthinking sacrilege.

Muir was persuaded to write in order to raise awareness, but it was not easy for him. As he later said, "Writing seems to me like the life of a glacier, one eternal grind."[46] But in the 1870s he produced over one hundred articles for leading magazines and newspapers across the country, perhaps the most famous of which was "God's First Temples," an 1876 contribution to the *Sacramento Daily Union*. Muir speaks of the forests and mountains as temples of the divine long before humanity was born.

But now, he said, they are being desecrated. In the nearby town of Fresno, for instance, already there were five lumber mills, and one of them alone had in one season processed over two million feet of sequoia. This was a ravaging of nature on a massive scale.

But Muir never simply denounced the ravaging. He also called on his readers to fall in love again with nature, and this is perhaps Muir's greatest prophetic gift to us today. He sets a pattern for us of resolutely denouncing the wrongs we are doing to the environment and at the same time invites us back into a love affair with the earth. It is the latter that will undergird and sustain a true relationship with the natural world.

He advises us to take time to be in the wilderness, promising that our "ancient mother-love" of nature will rise again.[47] We are to return to the mountains, he says, and we will be born anew. "Go back among the mountains and get their good tidings. . . . Winds will blow their freshness into you, and storms will give you new energy. . . . Nature's love will get into your heart as surely as sunshine into trees."[48] We do not have to create a love of nature in one another and in our society. Our work, rather, is to help reawaken the sense of the sacred that is already deep in the human soul, our primordial relationship with nature, our ancient mother love of the earth. We can be part of its rising again.

We should return to the mountains, says Muir, but not necessarily stay there. The great poets, philosophers, and prophets, like Jesus and Muhammad, he said, returned to the mountains again and again for inner strength and spiritual vision, but it was not in order to remain in the mountains. It was to descend from the mountains and call for change. "I wish I were so 'Sequoiacal,'" he writes, "that I could descend from these mountains like a John the Baptist to preach the green-brown woods to all the juiceless world . . . crying, 'Repent, for the Kingdom of Sequoia is at hand.'"[49] Well, this in a sense is exactly what Muir did, but not immediately.

In 1880, at the age of forty-two, he married Louisa Strentzel, whose family owned a twenty-five-hundred-acre fruit orchard in Martinez, California. Muir stopped writing to manage the farm for about ten years; the couple had two daughters, Wanda and Helen. Scholars have sometimes referred to this decade as his "lost years," but I believe they were among some of the most vital years in Muir's development. They grounded him, in a way that his own family upbringing had failed to do, in the sacredness of human interrelationship. When he reemerged in 1890 it was with a greater gravity of soul and voice.

After his decade of silence Muir wrote two enormously influential articles for *Century Magazine*, which had a readership of close to a million. He called nineteenth-century America back into right relationship with nature. People are beginning to find, he wrote, "that going to the mountains is going home; that wildness is a necessity; and that mountain parks and reservations are useful not only as fountains of timber and irrigating rivers, but as fountains of life."[50] Wildness is a necessity, he said, and so we must preserve it.

His 1890 articles made a powerful impact on the nation. By the end of the year Congress had established two national parks, Yosemite and Sequoia. This was only the beginning. For a nation to legislatively protect wilderness to this extent was unprecedented in the world. The contrast between nineteenth-century America, leading the way among nations in conservation legislation, and early twenty-first-century America, flouting international laws for the protection of the environment, is tragic. It is a tragedy that we must reverse if the planet as we have known it is to be saved. Muir gave much of the next decade of his life to writing and lobbying Washington for the protection of the nation's vast wildernesses. He had truly become John the Baptist of nature's sacredness.

In 1903 he accompanied President Theodore Roosevelt on a three-day camping expedition into Yosemite. These three days have been hailed by some as the most important conservation meeting in American history. During his presidency Roosevelt went on to establish 5 more national parks, 15 national nature reserves, 55 national bird sanctuaries and wildlife refuges, and 150 national forests. Muir's part in all of this was enormous.

But it was not all success for Muir, as it never is for a prophet. During the last ten years of his life he gave himself tirelessly to campaigning to save the Sierra Park Valley, also known as the Hetch Hetchy Valley, in Yosemite. The city of San Francisco wanted to dam up the valley as a water reservoir for the growing urban population. The angry Muir said this would be like damming up our cathedrals to turn them into water tanks.

The Hetch Hetchy protest was the first historical campaign of grassroots lobbying. But in the end it failed. Congress passed the Raker Act in 1913, allowing the city of San Francisco to build the dam and reservoir, effectively drowning one of Yosemite's most beautiful valleys. The loss is "hard to bear," wrote Muir. It "goes to my heart."[51]

Muir died the following year, 1914, on Christmas Eve, from pneumonia, aged seventy-six. He was heartbroken by the loss of Hetch Hetchy, but he remained a prophet of hope. "Earth has no sorrows," he wrote, "that Earth cannot heal."[52] These are words that speak also to this moment in time. The one fountain Soul, as Muir believed, is still within. It will not be stopped up. It still flows at the heart of the wildness of the natural world. Thus, there will be new beginnings for the earth. She will heal. The question is whether humanity will get to be part of that healing. Will we change quickly enough in our relationship with the earth to protect the future of our grandchildren and our grandchildren's children? Will we seize this moment for saving the world or will we miss it?

Muir's vision is being invoked today, because we need his vision more desperately now than ever. Muir Woods, Muir Beach, Muir College, Muir Glacier, the John Muir Way in Scotland, even a John Muir feast day on April 22 in the liturgical calendar of the Episcopal Church USA—these all witness to the ways in which his vision has been cherished among us.

After Muir's death in 1914 the editor of *Century Magazine*, Robert Underwood Johnson, wrote, "The world will look back to the time we live in and remember the voice of one crying in the wilderness and bless the name of John Muir."[53] That day is dawning for many. John Muir was not a perfect prophet. We do not bless him for his failings. We do, however, bless him for his powerful prophetic witness to the sacredness of the earth. His voice still lives among us, calling us to wake up to our relationship with the earth and to translate this awareness into urgent action for one another and the creatures. The time is ripe. The vision is strong and clear.

John Muir is an icon for us today of love for the earth, a love that led him to prophetically speak and act for it. Like all great prophets, he gave himself both to announcing what is true and denouncing what is false. He proclaimed the sacredness of the earth and condemned the sacrilege of the earth. He called on his readers to know the beauty of wilderness and warned them to protect that beauty. In all of this, he invited his contemporaries to fall in love again and again with nature.

Today we hear many voices denouncing the abuse of the environment. These are important voices, and it is imperative that we listen to them and their dire predictions of the catastrophes we are bringing on ourselves and future generations by continuing to wrong the earth. But these voices are always most powerful when they prophetically combine their condemnation of wrong with a call to love, a passionate anger at what is being done to the environment coupled inseparably with a passionate love for the earth. We need both. And we need to live and speak both. Muir says that deep within us is our primal love of the earth. This is the flame that will set us on fire, both to love and adore her and to cherish and honor her body.

Before concluding this chapter, I invite you to take a few minutes to pay attention to what Muir has awakened in you. As you do the reflection practice below, sitting in silence, name in gratitude what has been stirring within you from this chapter. (All of the meditative practices are collected in the appendix, which can be used on a daily basis to remain alert to what has been calling your inner attention as you read this book.)

REFLECTION: SACRED EARTH

WORDS OF AWARENESS

John Muir says that deep within the human soul is a primal love of the earth. We don't have to create or manufacture this love. Our role is simply to awaken to it again and release it in one another, so that together we may serve the earth with passion.

(Reflect for a brief time on the ways this wisdom applies to your life.)

PRAYER OF AWARENESS

Awake, O my soul,
And know that you are born of the earth.
Awake to your love for her,
Sown like a seed in the womb of your beginnings.
Honor her, protect her, cherish and adore her.
Awake, O my soul,
And know that you are born of the earth.

(Listen silently for a few minutes within the sacredness of your being.)

Awake, O my soul. Awake.

SACRED MATTER:
PIERRE TEILHARD DE CHARDIN

In the Celtic world, matter is sacred. So the matter of earth's body, including the human body, is cherished. It is in and through the stuff of the universe that we encounter the divine, in both its vastness and its intimacy.

In Chapter 1 we explored some of the earliest expressions of Celtic wisdom in ancient Gaul. In particular we heard how Irenaeus of Lyons in the second century taught that all things come out of the substance of God. This teaching powerfully articulated the Celtic awareness of matter as sacred. In the twentieth-century there was a resurrection of this early Gallic vision in the life and teachings of the French scientist, Jesuit priest, and mystic Pierre Teilhard de Chardin (1881–1955).

"At the heart of matter," said Teilhard, is "the heart of God."[1] The deeper we move in any created thing, the closer we approach the Life from which all life has come. "Let us leave the surface," wrote Teilhard, "and, without leaving the world, plunge into God."[2] When we experience the beat of this sacredness deep within us or encounter it in the body of the earth or the body of another, we have a sense of being addressed by name, said Teilhard. In other words, the life at the heart of all life is not just energy; it is presence. The universe is radically relational. In and through matter we are born for relationship, and at the heart of our relationship with the earth and one another is relationship with the divine.

As a result, Teilhard was able to pray, "O God . . . in the life which wells up in me and in the matter which sustains me, I find much more than your gifts. It is you yourself whom I find."[3] Teilhard rejects the dualism that has dominated Western thought. He refuses the divorce between spirit and matter that characterizes most of our philosophical and religious inheritance. The stuff of the universe is spirit-matter.

But this is not how Teilhard had been taught to view reality in his French Catholic upbringing. Rather, he had been educated to believe that matter is no more than "the humble servant" of spirit, if not "its enemy," he said.[4] He had been trained to suspect what is deep in the physical realm rather than revere it, including the deepest energies of our human sexuality. These might be subdued or harnessed to serve the spiritual, but they themselves were not regarded as sacred. Essentially, they were something other than God, and at worst opposed to God.

And yet Teilhard's earliest experiences of life were of being drawn to matter or, more specifically, as he describes it, "by something that shone at the heart of matter."⁵ Teilhard's childhood experience is not, I believe, unusual. Rather, he is pointing to something of which we can all remember glimpses of from childhood and our earliest experiences of light, dappling through the leaves of a tree, glistening green in the grasses, and shining clear in the currents of a river. The experience is of a universe flooded with light. What is unusual in Teilhard is that this childlike way of seeing continued into his adolescent and adult years. The world was on fire for him, ablaze. It was, he said, like a burning bush "lit from within."⁶

His traditional religious upbringing had not provided him with language for this way of seeing. Thus, as a young man, he became troubled by his attraction to the world. He found himself adoring the Light that is in all things, yet he feared that he was slipping into pantheism, in which everything is viewed as God.

Around the age of thirty, however, he had an epiphany in which he experienced himself being addressed by the Light that shines in matter. What he heard within himself were words from St. Matthew's Gospel, in Latin, *Ego sum, noli timere* ("It is I; do not be afraid" 14:27).⁷ He heard these words not from afar, as it were, or from above the physical, but from deep within the matter of the universe. The assurance that came to him in that moment was: "Do not be afraid to see matter as sacred; do not be afraid to adore this Light that is deep in all things. It is I."

"The universe," as Teilhard later wrote, now became "something that loved and could be loved."[8] His relationship with matter was now a love affair with the divine. He could freely adore the light that shines in the moon's light, for instance, or the light that glistens off flowing waters. He could love this light and, at the same time, know that he was being loved.

Previously he had thought there were only two choices, a love of heaven or a love of earth. Now a third path had opened for him, the realization that we are to "make our way to heaven through earth."[9] Now he saw it was through communion with the earth that we experience communion with God. This was not pantheism. Rather, it was the conviction that God is to be found *in* all things, a way of seeing called panentheism, as mentioned earlier.

Teilhard's experience of being addressed from deep within the universe with the words *ego sum, noli timere* brought to greater fullness for him his childhood awareness of something that shone at the heart of matter. He could now give himself to what on some level he had always adored. He prayed, "I love you, Lord Jesus, . . . you who are as gentle as the human heart, as fiery as the forces of nature, as intimate as life itself. . . . I love you as a world, as *this* world which has captivated my heart."[10]

When did Teilhard write these words: "I love you as a world, as *this* world which has captivated my heart"? It was at the battle of Dunkirk on Easter Day, 1916, where he was a stretcher bearer in the French army. These words were not an expression of romanticism spoken from the idyllic pastures of his boyhood in the Auvergne. They were uttered from the bloody trenches of World War I, in the midst of the horror of what humanity is capable of doing to itself and the earth.

Teilhard's love of the world was inseparable from his awareness of the world's sufferings. The Sacred Heart of Jesus devotion, in which the image of the pierced heart of Jesus is a symbol of divine love and which was so much part of his French Catholic upbringing, Teilhard now transferred to the heart of the universe. The sacred heart of the divine could be sought everywhere, in both the glory and the pain of the world.

By the 1920s Teilhard was prophetically announcing that a love of Christ and a love of the earth would be the "twin poles" of the Christianity of the future.[11] Love of Christ and love of creation, love of heaven and love of earth, love of spirit and love of matter—inseparably intertwined. "It is this," he writes, "I now see with a vision that will never leave me, that the world is desperately in need of at this very moment, if it is not to collapse."[12] One hundred years later these words speak into the heart of the present moment, perhaps more powerfully than ever. If the world as we know it is not to collapse, we need to reawaken to spirit shining in matter. We need not only to reawaken to this; we need also to live this awareness and serve it in one another and in the earth.

What the mystery of the Incarnation invites us to see, said Teilhard, is that we can be saved "only by becoming one with the universe."[13] The church's traditional doctrine of the Incarnation teaches that God was born in the flesh. Yet what has the church done with this radical teaching at the center of its faith? Instead of allowing it to point to the oneness of heaven and earth, the union of spirit and matter in all things, the marriage of the divine and the human in all people, the church has said that it is a truth that applies only to one, namely, Jesus, and that this one is an exception to humanity rather than a revelation of the deepest truth of humanity. The Light of the sacred is deep in all things. We will be well to the extent that we are one with this Light in one another and in the earth.

As we have already noted, the word *revelation* comes from the Latin *revelare*, which means "to lift the veil." In the Celtic world Jesus was seen as lifting the veil to show us what we have forgotten, which is not a foreign truth, but the most intimate of truths, the conjoining of heaven and earth deep in the matter of our being. This can be spoken of as our Christhood, a pure gift, given at birth, and waiting to grow into greater fullness in us. The great mystery of Christianity, said Teilhard, is not the appearance of God in the universe; it is "the transparence of God in the universe."[14] It is this that we are to reawaken to, spirit shining through matter everywhere. In the countenance of every human being, in the eyes of every creature, in the shining of every life-form, and in the depths of our own soul is the translucence through which we may glimpse the glory of heaven in earth.

Teilhard weaves into his prayers this interlacing of time and eternity, the physical and the spiritual, earth and heaven. He prays:

> *Matter, you in whom I find both seduction and strength,*
> *. . . you who can enrich and destroy, I surrender myself to*
> *your mighty layers with faith. . . . Let your attractions lead*
> *me forward, let your sap be the food that nourishes me. . . .*
> *Let your robberies and inroads [including even the inroad of*
> *death at the end] give me freedom. . . . Let your whole being*
> *lead me toward Godhead.*[15]

He was addressing matter! This was too much for Teilhard's ecclesiastical superiors. They summoned him to give account to the Jesuit provincial in Lyons, the irony of which cannot have escaped Teilhard, given Irenaeus of Lyons's teaching in the second century that all things come out of the substance of God. Teilhard wrote to a friend at this time: "They want me to promise in writing that I will never say or write anything against the traditional position of the Church on original sin."[16]

Teilhard was teaching so much more than mere opposition to the church's doctrine of original sin, in which it is taught that what is deepest in us, or most original in us, is opposed to God rather than of God. But his ecclesiastical superiors were right in sensing that Teilhard's vision was threatening the foundations of the church's theology, for if the doctrine of original sin is taken out of the theological edifice of imperial Christianity as it developed from the fourth century onward, the whole structure collapses. Every other doctrine can be seen to rest on this cornerstone.

But the conflict was much bigger than the doctrine of original sin itself. As Teilhard said to the same friend, we need to free our religion "from everything about it that is specifically Mediterranean."[17] And by "Mediterranean" he meant imperial. He meant the whole system of Western Christian thought that had its origins in the relationship between power and religion, the alliance between the might of the fourth-century Roman Empire and its adopted religion, Christianity. It was at this point historically that Christianity began to serve power. It was employed to tell people what to believe rather than awakening them to their deepest sensibilities of the sacredness of the earth and every birth.

As Teilhard wrote in 1921, "The Church is still a child. Christ, by whom she lives, is immeasurably greater than she imagines."[18] Teilhard saw that no boundaries are to be set on the Christ mystery, by which he meant the conjoining of heaven and earth, the marriage of spirit and matter, which is everywhere present. This mystery is not for the benefit only of one power group or one religion or for the blessing only of those whom empire and church find it convenient to bless. This mystery is for the blessing of all, for it is the mystery at the heart of all life, all matter.

In 1926 the Vatican forbade Teilhard from teaching and writing theologically. Instead, he was sent on a scientific expedition to China to work as a paleontologist in an archaeological dig. This, thought the Vatican, would deal with the inconvenience of Teilhard!

But little did the Vatican know what the East would do to this Gallic prophet of earth's sacredness. In China he began to speak not only about the sacredness of matter, but also the sacredness of the feminine. The "fragrance" of the feminine, as he called it, or "the world's attractive power," is that dimension deep within us and deep within the matter of the universe that invites union.[19]

By union, Teilhard means the oneness of interrelatedness. He does not mean uniformity or conformity. One of the guiding principles in both his scientific work and his spiritual teaching is that true union differentiates. This is what we know in the realm of scientific observation. The oneness of the universe keeps producing greater and greater multiplicity, more and more differentiation of life-forms. Similarly, we know this in the most intimate relationships of our lives. The people who truly love us, and are thus most deeply one with us, are the people who have the capacity to most radically set us free to be ourselves. They delight in the uniqueness of our heart and mind, our body and soul; everything in us is cherished by everything in them. True union gives birth to the glory of differentiation.

The fragrance of the feminine, of which Teilhard speaks, invites union; it is an attractive power that expresses itself in and through the very matter of the universe. The universal law of gravitation is a manifestation of this power of attraction. At some level every atom in the cosmos longs to remain in relationship with every other atom. Otherwise the whole thing would spin off into unrelatedness. This law of attraction is at work within us, both physically and spiritually. We can awaken to it within ourselves and honor it in the relationships of our lives and world. It has the power to bring us, both individually and collectively, back into faithful relationship with the earth and one another as nations and races and religions, that we may know again the oneness that radically affirms uniqueness.

There had been important feminine influences in Teilhard's life. In his cousin Marguerite Teillard-Chambon he had experienced the faithfulness of the feminine in a deep and abiding friendship that brought an assurance within him that he would always be loved, a gift beyond measure. Now in China he encountered the artistic and sensuous feminine in Lucile Swan, an American sculptress and portrait painter living in Peking. For ten years they saw each other almost every day, either in the privacy of her home or walking together on the Great Wall or in the botanical gardens of the imperial city.

Teilhard found in Lucile what he called the "spiritual fertility" of the feminine.[20] By this he meant her ability to help conceive new consciousness in him. During a brief time apart he wrote to her saying, "So many things I have to keep to myself now, and so many things . . . do not get born in my mind because you are not here to give me . . . the internal impetus."[21] Once again we see the importance of what in the Celtic Christian world from the earliest centuries had been called the *anamchara* relationship, having a friend or lover of the soul whose very presence calls forth what is stirring in our depths, longing to come up into consciousness. Lucile was the lover of Teilhard's soul. She released in him what he had not yet been able to articulate.

But the relationship with Lucile was not uncomplicated. She longed for complete oneness with Teilhard, including sexual union. She wrote to him:

Please don't think I mean just sex, although that is very strong. It would make a bond between us that would add a strength that I believe nothing else can give. However, that is only a part. I want to be with you when you are well and when you are ill. Go see beautiful things with you and walk through the country. In other words, I want to stand beside you always, to laugh and play and pray with you. Don't you

realize what a big part of life that is, and how that is what is
right and natural and God-given.[22]

We don't know the exact nature of their relationship, and we don't need to know. World War II parted them, and they never lived in the same place again.

But, importantly, we *do* know that Teilhard was not frightened by this power of attraction. Even before China, he had heard the voice of the sacred within himself saying, "I am at . . . the heart of your own being and of all things, to welcome even the wildest of your longings and to assure you that not one single fragment of what is useful in them will be lost to God."[23] Let us not be frightened by the longings that stir within us for the earth and for one another. Let us rather pray that not one single fragment of what is useful in them will be lost in the great work of bringing all things back into relationship.

Within us, believed Teilhard, is the world's attractive power. It is given to serve love, the greatest energy of the human mystery. "Love alone," he said, "is capable of uniting living beings in such a way as to complete and fulfill them, for it alone takes them and joins them by what is deepest in themselves."[24] At the wedding feast of dear friends in France, Teilhard articulated his vision of a world that could be changed by love. Elsewhere he had called it the "amorization" of the universe.[25] He did not mean only romantic love. In the vows through which these friends were wholly giving themselves to each other in body and soul, heart and mind, he saw a sacrament of the love that is longing to come forth from the true depths of every human being. This capacity for love in the human soul is what can reunite us to the sacred that is deep in all things. "The core of every living creature," said Teilhard, is "its power to love."[26]

Teilhard prophesied that the day will come when, after harnessing all the energies of earth, sea, and sky, humanity will finally learn how to harness its greatest energy, love. On that day, he said, we will have "discovered fire" for the second time.[27]

After the war Teilhard returned to Paris. Once again, he became an inconvenience for those in power. There were radical implications to teaching the sacredness of matter as well as the sacredness of the feminine and its power to break through barriers that have been used to separate us from each other. Teilhard's teachings challenged religion with regard to where the sacred is to be sought and adored, and they challenged the power structures of the Western world in relation to the way matter is to be handled. Any sympathy that Teilhard might have enjoyed at one stage with the leadership of the church in France was strained by the reports that had already reached Europe about the sorts of things he had been saying in China; such as, we need to "save Christ from the hands of the clergy so that the world may be saved."[28]

His presence in Europe was again too much for his superiors.

The Vatican decided he must be sent again into exile, this time to that other remote outpost of humanity, the United States of America!

Teilhard was dispatched to New York City. There he took up residence at the Jesuit house of St. Ignatius Loyola on Park Avenue, although often he was abroad on paleontological digs in South Africa and elsewhere, literally digging into the matter of the earth as he delved also into the depths of the human soul for truth.

In his spiritual writings, none of which were allowed by the Vatican to be published, Teilhard had spoken of the sacredness of matter and the sacredness of the feminine. During his American exile he now began to speak of the sacredness of sacrifice. What love prompts us to do, he believed, is to lose ourselves in love and thereby truly find ourselves, to live not from our false self, driven by the ego, but from our true self, made of God. This was not to disparage the ego and our faculties of consciousness and willpower. Rather, it was to say that our ego has been created not to *be* the center, but to *serve* the center, not to focus on itself, but to focus on the sacredness at the heart of one another and all things.

For Teilhard the sacredness of sacrifice has nothing to do with the doctrine of expiation for sin that has so dominated much of Western Christianity's understanding of the sacrifice of Christ.

For Teilhard, love's redemptive work is about turning sin into new beginnings and in that sense redeeming sin. It is about allowing the failures of life, whether individual or collective, to be the occasion for seeking forgiveness and reconciliation, thus enabling the wrongs we have committed or experienced to become the very seedbed from which new beginnings may arise.

We urgently need to develop a "new" meaning of the cross, said Teilhard.[29] Many in the Christian world today and great numbers beyond it are astounded, and even appalled, by a religion that continues in its language and symbolism to suggest that God somehow required the death of Jesus in order to forgive humanity, in other words expiation for the forgiveness of sin. At the core of our being we know this cannot be true, for it violates our deepest experiences of how love works. Could we imagine, for instance, those who have most loved us in our lives needing to be paid to forgive us? It contradicts what we most deeply know of love. Teilhard and other teachers in this great stream of wisdom help us remember that although sacrifice is costly, it is never about payment for love. It is about offering ourselves, including even our failures, in the holy service of love and new beginnings.

Together, said Teilhard, we are to bear the weight of the world in its journey of unfolding. We have the ability to respond to the sins of our nations and religions and the many personal failures of our own making. We have the ability to confess, to name and repent of what we have done to the earth and one another, and to allow these failings thus to be turned into the stuff of new beginnings. We have response-ability. Will we take it up? The earth is "groaning in labor pains," as the Christian scriptures say (Rom. 8:22). A price has to be paid for the labor, says Teilhard. Are we willing to take on the pangs of new birthing? This is the question before us. It is the urgency of love's sacrificial work.

Sacrifice is not about ceasing to love oneself. That would be "absurd," says Teilhard. Nor is it about loving oneself less. That would be "pernicious." Rather, sacrifice is about loving oneself "in a different and better way," he says.[30] It is about shifting the axis of our life outside of ourselves. It is about decentering ourselves or what he calls "ex-centration," by which he means "the radical sacrifice of egoism," finding our true center not within the limited confines of our own individuality, but at the center of one another and of everything that has being.[31]

There is a tremendous spiritual power slumbering in the human soul, says Teilhard. It will come forth again when we learn "to break down the barriers of our egoisms."[32] And it is not just about our personal ego; it is also about the ego of our nation, our religion, our class, and our race. Teilhard writes:

> *In your excessive self-love, you are like a molecule closed in upon itself and incapable of entering easily into any new combination. . . . Have done, then, with your egoism and your fear of suffering. Love others as you love yourself, that*

is to say, admit them into yourself, all of them. . . . Take up your cross, my soul.[33]

Elsewhere Teilhard calls this the "primacy of humility," learning to live from the sacred common ground of life rather than lifting ourselves up over one another or separating ourselves from one another.[34]

These are not just *words* from Teilhard. He was also *living* the sacredness of sacrifice. Teilhard was a teacher and a writer, and yet his own tradition had silenced him, preventing him from doing what he most loved and felt called to do. He responded not by serving his ego, but by trying to be a faithful son of his religious tradition. When, at the promptings of friends, he finally agreed to an act of disobedience, it was not, I believe, out of self-love, but out of love for the world, which had so captured his heart. In 1951 he signed over all of his writings, none of which the Vatican had allowed to be published, to Jeanne Mortier, his personal assistant in Paris. This meant that upon his death his writings would be hers, not the church's.

Teilhard died on Easter Day, 1955, relatively unknown. Ten people attended his funeral in the chapel of the Jesuit house on Park Avenue, and only one person accompanied his body from New York City to the Jesuit graveyard in Poughkeepsie, up the Hudson River.

In the following years his writings were released, one at a

time, by Mademoiselle Mortier. The Vatican responded by forbidding Teilhard's works from being retained in church libraries and educational institutions. His books were not to be sold in Catholic bookstores or translated into other languages. The church hierarchy warned its religious teachers of the need to protect the minds, especially of the young, "against the dangers presented by the works of Teilhard de Chardin and his followers."[35] But the ban did not work. As Teilhard himself had said, no truth "has ever been conquered by repression."[36] And, as we have seen again and again over the centuries in imperial Christianity's attempts to silence Celtic prophets, bans never work against what the soul deeply knows to be true.

I still meet priests and religious sisters today who were training in the late 1950s. They have memories of reading Teilhard's books by flashlight under the covers in bed at night and strapping his publications under their mattresses by day. This is exactly what true spiritual writing needs to be. It needs to be so exciting and related to the unfolding journey of humanity that we will read it no matter who tells us not to, for in reading it we will know that some of the deepest yearnings of our soul are being nurtured.

During one of my most recent trips to New York City, when I was teaching briefly at Iona College in New Rochelle, the director of their Institute for Earth and Spirit, Sister Kathleen Deignan, offered to take me on a pilgrimage to Teilhard's grave. The property around it is now owned by the Culinary Institute of America, so, in order to access the graveyard, we needed to obtain a key from security. It was a rainy day in April and, although we were ill clad for the weather, we knelt by the grave to give thanks.

Praying with Kathleen in the rain at the grave of Pierre Teilhard de Chardin was an experience I shall never forget. We began by taking it in turn to pray. Kathleen then moved from prayer into direct address to Teilhard, calling him "teacher," "master," "prophet."

At the end of our thanksgiving, still kneeling at the grave, she said, "I just love him. I'd like to get down into that box and give him a hug."

"I love Teilhard as well," I said to Kathleen, "but that is not what I want to do!"

So, instead, we agreed to enjoy some French cuisine in the Culinary Institute of America and raise a glass of Bordeaux in honor of Teilhard, the great modern Gallic prophet.

But first, on our way out of the graveyard, we had to return the key. "Do many people visit Teilhard's grave?" I asked the receptionist.

"Oh, yes," she replied. "Every day, dozens."

Teilhard was a prophet, speaking well ahead of his time, right into the heart of this moment.

In one of his last writings, Teilhard said, Christianity "is reaching the end of one of the natural cycles of its existence. . . . After what will soon be two thousand years, Christ must be born again."[37] In that born-again Christianity, he said, Christ will no longer be seen as a deserter of the earth. He will be seen as a lover of the earth, at one with the earth.

At the heart of our being and at the heart of all being is the beat of the divine. We do not have to invoke or summon it from afar. It is here and now, always here, always now. The invitation is simply to awaken to the sacred, to open to it, and in knowing it deep within us to know that we are part of it, and in being part of it to know also that we are part of one another and of everything in the cosmos, the sacred interrelationship of all being. "All we have to do," said Teilhard, "is let the very heart of the earth beat within us."[38]

Teilhard is an icon for us today of being alive to the sacredness of matter. Teilhard's awareness led him to defy a system that was neglecting or even denying this sacredness. Although silenced by his ecclesiastical superiors and forbidden to publish, he courageously continued to write. But before he died, Teilhard, in an act of priestly disobedience, signed over all of his writings for publication after his death. This was a courageous act, to oppose the leadership of the tradition that he had given his life to.

Our English word *courage* is derived from the old French *corage*, based on the word *coeur*, which means "heart." *Cor-age,* or *coeur*-age, is about living from the heart, and it is in the heart that love resides, our greatest strength.

We need courage, strength of heart, if we are to be part of the holy work of reawakening to the sacredness of matter. Some of our courageous work may take place on the big stage of helping to move organizations and nations in the direction of honoring the matter of the earth and the matter of human lives. But all of us are also called to be people of courage in the more humble and often unnoticed realms of family life and work, even in how we look at one another and personally behave, how we heat our houses, or how we resource and prepare our food. To reverence the sacredness of matter often means courageously opposing the norms of society and government policies. Like Teilhard, we need to draw from our heart in this work, our place of inner strength and love.

Before concluding this chapter, I invite you to take a few minutes to pay attention to what Teilhard has awakened in you. As you do the reflection practice below, sitting in silence, name in gratitude what has been stirring within you from this chapter. (All of the meditative practices are collected in the appendix, which can be used on a daily basis to remain alert to what has been calling your inner attention as you read this book.)

Reflection: Sacred Matter

Words of Awareness

Pierre Teilhard de Chardin awakens us to the sacredness of matter. The body of the earth, including the human body, has a translucence through which the Light of the divine can be glimpsed. At the heart of matter is the heart of God.

(*Reflect for a brief time on the ways this wisdom applies to your life.*)

Prayer of Awareness

Awake, O my soul,
To the sacred stream of light that runs through you.
Awake to it in the body of the earth and every life-form,
In the moist fecundity of valleys
And the hard matter of mountain granite,
All things in flux and further becoming.
Awake, O my soul,
To the sacred stream of light that runs through you.

(*Listen silently for a few minutes within the sacredness of your being.*)

Awake, O my soul. Awake.

SACRED COMPASSION:
GEORGE MACLEOD

To know that spirit and matter are interwoven, that heaven and earth, the divine and the human are inseparably intertwined, is to know also that what we do to matter matters. In the Celtic world, to adore the divine is to reverence the human, to love heaven is to cherish the earth, and to celebrate spirit is to honor matter. And it is to do all these things with compassion, by bringing the heart of our being into faithful relationship with the heart of one another's being and allowing the sacred interrelationship of all things to guide us and to inspire us in how we live and act.

George Fielden MacLeod (1895–1991) was a Celtic prophet in twentieth-century Scotland who lived the way of compassion. He saw that the spiritual is to be found deep in the physical and that heaven is to be served in the material needs of humanity and the earth. Spirituality therefore took the form of caring for the planet and for the lives of families struggling with homelessness, illness, and hunger in the slums of Scottish cities and communities throughout the world. For MacLeod it also took the form of nonviolence, not only nonviolence of action but also nonviolence of heart.[1]

What a wonderful world this is, he said, provided we believe in another world not over against this world but interlaced with it. The air of the eternal is "seeping through the physical," said MacLeod.[2] How we touch and care for the stuff of the body of the earth and the body of humanity, therefore, is how we touch and care for the divine.

Part of MacLeod's greatness is that he didn't mind repeating himself. He lived until he was ninety-six, so he had plenty of opportunity—and he did so shamelessly! MacLeod's repeated sayings were like mantras of his core beliefs. "Matter matters," he would say—the matter of the body of the earth, the matter of the human body, and the matter of the body politic. This was the heart of his vision.

And if you were to meet him on the High Street in Edinburgh or on a quiet pathway on Iona, you would tend to get not "Good morning" or "How are you today?" but "Do you believe in nonviolence?" He would ask it with such assertiveness that you felt terrified to disagree. MacLeod was perhaps the most aggressive pacifist the modern world has known!

But it wasn't always, "Do you believe in nonviolence?" In a nation that was the home of Presbyterianism, it was sometimes the much more playful question, "Are you a Presbyterian or a Christian?" MacLeod was forever challenging the definitions we use to describe ourselves. Always he wanted his listeners to think again about the boxes into which we have placed ourselves when we speak about nations, races, and religions.

George MacLeod is best known for the rebuilding of the abbey on the island of Iona off the western coast of Scotland. He saw it as a rebuilding of the spirituality of St. Columba and the Celtic Christian vision that had taken root in Scotland in the sixth century. One of MacLeod's greatest prayers from the rebuilding years on Iona is modeled on *The Breastplate Hymn of St. Patrick*, in which Christ is sought in all things:

> *Christ above us, Christ beneath us,*
> *Christ beside us, Christ within us.*
>
> *Invisible we see you, Christ above us.*
> *With earthly eyes we see above us clouds or sunshine,*
> *grey or bright.*
> *But with the eye of faith, we know you . . .*
> *instinct in the sun ray,*
> *speaking in the storm,*
> *warming and moving all creation, Christ above us.*
>
> *Invisible we see you, Christ beneath us.*
> *With earthly eyes we see beneath us stones and dust*
> *and dross, . . .*
> *But with the eye of faith, we know you uphold.*
> *In you all things consist and hang together:*

The very atom is light energy,
　　the grass is vibrant,
　　the rocks pulsate.
All is in flux; turn but a stone and an angel moves.
Underneath are the everlasting arms.
Unknowable we know you, Christ beneath us.

Inapprehensible we know you, Christ beside us.
With earthly eyes we see men and women, exuberant or dull,
　　tall or small.
But with the eye of faith, we know you dwell in each.
You are imprisoned in . . . the dope fiend and the drunk,
dark in the dungeon, but you are there.
You are released, resplendent, in the loving mother,
. . . the passionate bride,
and in every sacrificial soul.
Inapprehensible we know you, Christ beside us.

Intangible, we touch you, Christ within us.
With earthly eyes we see ourselves, dust of the dust, earth of
　　the earth.
But with the eye of faith, we know ourselves all girt about of
　　eternal stuff,
　　our minds capable of divinity,
　　our bodies groaning, waiting for the revealing,

our souls redeemed, renewed.
Intangible we touch you, Christ within us.

Christ above us, beneath us, beside us, within us, what need
  have we for temples made with hands?[3]

When MacLeod uses the word "Christ" he is pointing not just to the historical figure of Jesus Christ but to the conjoining of heaven and earth, the divine and the human, spirit and matter, which is to be looked for everywhere and in everyone. "We have been given union with God," he said, "whether we like it or not, know it or not, want it or not. Our flesh is . . . [God's] flesh and we can't jump out of our skins."[4]

This vision was not part of MacLeod's immediate upbringing, although it is interesting to note that his grandfather, Norman MacLeod, had been a disciple of Alexander John Scott, the nineteenth-century Celtic prophet of the imagination whose work we explored in Chapter 5. George MacLeod's father, Sir John MacLeod, on the other hand, was a member of Parliament for Glasgow Central and the chief recruiting officer of the British army in Scotland during World War I. The young MacLeod grew up as a son of the Scottish aristocracy, with maids in his family home and printed menus for evening meals. He attended one of the most exclusive

schools for boys in Britain, Winchester College in England, before
going on to study at Oxford. After university he became an officer in the British army, fighting in the trenches of France during
World War I. For his bravery at the front he was decorated with the
Croix de Guerre and the Military Cross, two of the highest military awards.

The turning point for MacLeod, however, came toward the end
of the war when he was traveling back from the front lines in a train
full of soldiers, many of whom were wounded. Halfway through
the journey MacLeod became aware of the presence of Christ, not
somehow above or beyond the suffering that surrounded him but
in the midst of its pain and brokenness. Being a man of action, Mac-
Leod did not wait until the end of the train journey to respond. He
knelt down where he was in the crowded railway carriage and gave
himself to Christ. This led him forever afterward to be looking for
the divine in both the suffering and the glory of humanity and the
earth. "Christ is vibrant," he said, "in the material world, not just in
the spiritual world."[5] And to seek the divine in matter is to look for
it in places both of beauty and of agony in the world.

After the war MacLeod trained for the Church of Scotland
ministry and then became assistant minister at St Giles' in Edinburgh, Scotland's national cathedral. His remarkable oratorical
and poetic gifts led him to become a rising star in the ministry of
the Scottish Church. MacLeod's prayers were distillations of his
vision, and he would labor over them, constantly refining them,
for hours before delivering them:

Almighty God . . .
Sun behind all suns,
soul within all souls . . .
Show to us in everything we touch and in everyone we meet
the continued assurance of thy presence round us,
lest ever we should think thee absent.
In all created things thou art there.
In every friend we have
the sunshine of thy presence is shown forth.
In every enemy that seems to cross our path,
thou art there within the cloud
to challenge us to love.
Show to us the glory in the grey.
Awake for us thy presence in the very storm
till all our joys are seen as thee
and all our trivial tasks emerge as priestly sacraments
in the universal temple of thy love.[6]

It was thought that MacLeod could have any pulpit in Scotland, so widely was he admired for his gifts of preaching and public prayer. But in 1930 he shocked the religious establishment by accepting a call to the poorest parish, Govan Old, in Glasgow, ravaged at the time by economic depression and massive unemployment. It was here that he began to speak of the two nations of Scotland, the nation of the rich and the nation of the poor.

"What really is the gospel?" he asked:

> *Is it really the declaration of a spiritual world over against a*
> *material world? . . . Is it that the physical, the earthly, is of*
> *very passing account whether it be physical bodies, or . . . the*
> *bodies-politic, and that matter does not matter, while spirit*
> *matters everything? I just cannot find it in the Bible.*[7]

What MacLeod found in the scriptures is that it is precisely in the material realm that the divine is to be found. Christ, he said, came in a body and healed bodies and fed bodies. He came to save us body and soul. In other words, for MacLeod it was the material interwoven with the spiritual. It was about caring for our body-souls and the body-soul of the earth and all people.

MacLeod taught the holiness of wholeness. Holiness, he said, is essentially about "healthiness."[8] It is about healthy relationship with the earth and one another as individuals, communities, and nations. The words *holy* and *whole* are derived from the same root, the Middle English word *hale*, which means "health." The pursuit of holiness is the pursuit of healthiness in our lives and world. It is not soul salvation, he would say; it is whole salvation, for we are not called to be escape artists. We are not called to seek liberation from the world, but a liberation of the world. The time of salvation is here and now, for healing must be here and now. *Salve* means "healing ointment." To be part of salv-ation is to be part of healing in the world, of bringing what is torn and infected among us back into health and relationship again.

MacLeod loved to tell the story of a boy who had been throwing stones at a stained-glass window of the Incarnation in a city church. At the base of the window were inscribed the words, "GLORY TO GOD IN THE HIGHEST." The boy's stone nicked out the letter "E" in the word "HIGHEST," so the inscription read "GLORY TO GOD IN THE HIGH ST," which, said MacLeod, is exactly how it should be left, if not with a swiveling panel for the letter E so that it could say both.[9] The glory of God was to be looked for everywhere, on the streets of our cities and in the most ordinary matters and struggles of daily life.

"It is precisely the conjunction of the vertical and the horizontal," MacLeod said, "that makes the Cross."[10] At-one-ment is where the lines meet. The work of Christhood is about the intersection of the two, heaven and earth, the divine and the human, spirit and matter. He said:

> *I am recovering the claim that Jesus was not crucified in a cathedral between two candlesticks but on a cross between two thieves . . . at a crossroad so cosmopolitan that they had to write his title in Hebrew and in Latin and in Greek . . . because that is where he died. And that is what he died about.*[11]

Jesus died in being faithful to the union of the divine and the human, the spiritual and the physical. That, contended MacLeod, is what frightens power—when we do the work of challenging how matter is handled. The trouble with the church today, he said, is that nobody wants to persecute it. This, he believed, is because Christianity is not doing the radical work of honoring the marriage of spirit and matter in our lives and world.

This was not just activism for MacLeod. This was mystical vision combined with compassionate action. Prayerful awareness in every moment of life is what he taught. "The primacy of God as now," he said, is what we must recover as the starting point of a new holiness. "Our innumerable and pedestrian 'nows' are our points of contact with God."[12] It is not as if the spiritual is some separate category of life that relates in a limited way to prayer and spiritual practice. The divine is to be sought at the heart of every moment, every place, and every encounter.

MacLeod recounted the poignant story of his daughter's first day of school:

I was busy. I was writing letters. I was self-important. My little daughter was going to school that morning for the first time. She came into my room, in her first school uniform. I said, "Your tie is not quite straight." Then I looked at her eyes. She wasn't crying. She was unutterably disappointed. She hadn't come for tie inspection. She had come to show she was going to school for the first time. A terrific day, and I had let her down. What is that bit in the Gospel? Whosoever shall offend against one of these little ones

> *. . . better for a millstone to be tied around his neck and*
> *that he be cast into the sea. I ran downstairs. I said all the*
> *right things. I crossed the road with her. I went to school*
> *with her. But I had missed the moment, missed the point. I*
> *will always see these eyes. Sometimes when I am very busy.*
> *Sometimes when I am writing letters. I am forgiven, but*
> *I won't forget.*[13]

A universal story of missing the moment, missing the point.

It is a mistaken belief, said MacLeod, that "to go mystical" is to somehow turn away from the affairs of the world.[14] Rather, for MacLeod, to go mystical was to move more deeply into the affairs of the world and into the most ordinary matters of everyday life. So, in 1938, as the world prepared for war, MacLeod was preparing to build a community of radical nonviolence.

In 1938, along with unemployed craftsmen and theological students, MacLeod began to rebuild the domestic buildings of Iona Abbey. For him it was a symbol of rebuilding the spirituality of Columba, whose name in Gaelic was Columcille, meaning "Dove of the Church." To rebuild was to prophetically recover the foundations of a spirituality of nonviolence that would honor the spiritual and the physical as one.

But Europe was preparing for war. It was a difficult time to raise funds for the reconstruction of a medieval abbey. Fifty years later I heard MacLeod speak about his first fundraising efforts in 1938. "I wrote to the three wealthiest men I knew," he said, "asking them each for £5000. I still haven't heard back from the first man," he laughed. "The second man sent me the name and address of his psychiatrist. And the third man was Sir James Lithgow, a shipbuilding magnate in the Clyde who was building naval vessels for the Ministry of Defense."

Sir James Lithgow invited MacLeod to a meeting over lunch. At the beginning of the meal Lithgow pulled a check out of his pocket and said, "MacLeod, if I give you this £5000, will you give up your pacifism?"

MacLeod declined.

Lithgow immediately replied, "In that case, here is the £5000. I wouldn't have given it to you if you had given up your principles."

So, effectively, it was money from the Ministry of Defense that enabled MacLeod to work on rebuilding the spiritual foundations of nonviolence in Scotland.

It was during these early years on Iona that MacLeod, inspired by the landscape and seascape of the Hebrides, wrote a prayer in which he speaks of knowing the glory of eternity in time as well as our age-old struggle to be true to this union of spirit and matter:

Almighty God . . .
the morning is yours, rising into fullness.

The summer is yours, dipping into autumn.

Eternity is yours, dipping into time.

The vibrant grasses, the scent of flowers, the lichen on the
   rocks, the tang of seaweed,

All are yours.

Gladly we live in this garden of your creating.

. . . [yet] in the garden also

always the thorn. . . .

In the garden that is each of us, always the thorn.[15]

For MacLeod the thorn was particularly violence, both individual and collective, the hatred that infects our heart and can tear apart the relationships of our lives and world.

At first the British Broadcasting Company was enchanted by this Celtic prophet and loved his vision of a rebuilt Iona Abbey. BBC World Service covered his sermons live. His voice was being heard all over the world from a remote island in Scotland. People sometimes wondered how it was that, when MacLeod entered the pulpit to preach, seagulls on Iona could be heard cawing outside, as if in response to the great man. The simple explanation is that MacLeod had instructed his assistants to scatter fish on the abbey grounds at the beginning of his sermon. He was a great visionary— and also a great schemer!

In 1939, however, with the outbreak of war, he was silenced, and for the next six years the BBC covered not a single word of

MacLeod's. The British Empire at war did not want its people to be taught by a prophet of nonviolence. Fundraising became even more difficult for him, as did locating supplies for the rebuilding of the abbey. In later years MacLeod delighted in recounting the almost unbelievable stories of how building resources kept finding their way to Iona during the war. In particular he loved the story of how on one storm-tossed night an oceangoing vessel carrying Canadian timber got into trouble off the Atlantic coastline of Iona. The ship was forced to jettison its cargo, which washed up immediately opposite Iona on the shores of Mull. And as MacLeod would add with a twinkle in his eyes, "It was all exactly the right length!" Then he would say, "And if you think that's a coincidence, may you live a very boring life!"

But the reconstruction of the abbey was never an end in itself for MacLeod. It was always also a sign of the need to rebuild the vision of matter conjoined with spirit and thus the imperative of caring for the earth and for the matter of human lives and relationships:

> It is not just the interior of these walls:
> it is our own inner beings you have renewed.

> We are your temple not made with hands.
> We are your body.
> If every wall should crumble and every church decay,

we are your habitation.
Nearer are you than breathing, closer than hands and feet.
Ours are the eyes with which you, in the mystery,
look out in compassion on the world.

So we bless you for this place.
For your directing of us, your redeeming of us, and your
  indwelling.
Take us "outside the camp," Lord.
Outside holiness.
Out to where soldiers gamble,
and thieves curse,
and nations clash
at the cross-roads of the world. . . .
So shall this building continue to be justified.[16]

MacLeod spoke of Iona as a "thin place," a place where the distinction between heaven and earth, the spiritual and the physical, is only thinly veiled. But he did not thereby mean that every other place was "thick." Iona for him was a sacrament or an icon through which we glimpse the thinness that is everywhere present. Time on Iona was not an escape from the challenging places of our lives where it is more difficult to see and to serve the sacredness of the physical. Rather, the grace of Iona for MacLeod was that it is a place where we more readily awaken to the oneness of heaven and earth, so that we may be strengthened for the holy work of serving that union everywhere.

MacLeod was on Iona on August 6, 1945, the day the atom bomb was dropped on Hiroshima. He later reflected on that moment:

> *Suppose the material order, as we have argued, is indeed the garment of Christ, the Temple of the Holy Spirit? . . . Then what is the atom but the emergent body of Christ? . . .*
>
> *The Feast of the Transfiguration is August 6th. That is the day when we "happened" to drop the bomb at Hiroshima. We took God's body and we took God's blood and we enacted a cosmic Golgotha. We took the key to love and we used it for bloody hell.*
>
> *Nobody noticed. I am not being cheap about other people. I did not notice it myself. I was [on Iona] celebrating the Feast of the Transfiguration, in a gown and a cassock, a hood, a stole, white hands, saying with the whole Christian ministry, "This is my body, . . . this is my blood."*
>
> *Meanwhile our "Christian civilization," without Church protest, made its assertion of the complete divorce between spirit and matter.*
>
> *One man noticed. When the word came through to Washington of the dropping of the atom bomb—"Mission accomplished"—Dr. Oppenheimer, in large degree in our*

name its architect, was heard to say, "Today the world has seen sin."[17]

The word *sin* comes from the Old High German *sunda*, which means "to sunder or tear apart." For MacLeod the sundering forces of darkness in the world are so powerful, both within us and between us, that we need more than the strength of our ego to confront them, including the ego of our nation. What we need to access, said MacLeod, is the mighty realm of angelic strength, by which he meant the sacred energies of light that flood the universe and are accessible within us and between us, both individually and together:

> *The cry should not be "back to the angels" but "forward to the angels."... We must recover the ancient insight that all forces [in the universe] are ultimately personal, all its motions ultimately directed in the service of love.... People do not speak of angels today. But behold! They do not hesitate to speak of things demonic.... [We] have lost the key to the consciousness of angels again.... God grant that it will be given to us to see the return of Michael or, if not to us, to our children: or, if not to them, to our children's children, to see the return of Michael. This time not to temples made with hands: but to this emergent universal temple of earth and sky and sea.*[18]

The task of confronting the destructive forces of fear and violence is great. We need more than ego strength to combat them. We need the mightiest forces of the divine—love and compassion. These are the sacred energies of light that are within us and that we can draw on in our lives and world.

After the war the rebuilding continued. Iona was now becoming a place of international pilgrimage. For MacLeod it was a platform from which to address the nation and the world. By the late 1940s he was prophetically announcing the coming environmental crisis and calling for organic farming. In the second half of the twentieth century, as ecological consciousness gained more and more prominence in the Western world, MacLeod described it as humanity becoming "earthed" again.[19] Surely the role of the church, he said, is to emphatically proclaim that this is precisely where God is to be found, in the matter of the earth and in humanity's relationship to it.

Iona had become a place of international interest, but the community that MacLeod founded in rebuilding the abbey continued its focus on the particular challenges of Scotland's inner cities, namely, hunger, housing, and justice. MacLeod became a leading national voice in the Campaign for Nuclear Disarmament. He was both loved and hated for his prophetic stance, but was gradually recognized at least by some within the religious and political establishment of Britain when in 1956 he was appointed Scottish Chaplain to the queen. In 1968 Queen Elizabeth honored him with a lordship. He was now Lord MacLeod of Fuinary and the first member of the Green Party to sit in the House of Lords. Typically, in response to such honors, MacLeod said that this all went to show that he never was a real prophet!

Year after year he would urge the General Assembly of the Church of Scotland to call on the British government to disarm itself of nuclear weapons, and year after year the assembly would vote MacLeod down. One year a good friend suggested to him that he speak in favor of nuclear arms. That way, said his friend, the assembly, which always voted against MacLeod on this issue, would immediately defeat his motion and thus end up affirming the movement for nuclear disarmament! MacLeod did in fact live to see the day when the General Assembly of the Church of Scotland called on the British government to unilaterally disarm itself of weapons of mass destruction. It was the assembly of May 1982.

Prophetically MacLeod was critical of religious irrelevance and called for radical change, but never did he contemplate leaving the church. In a prayer in which he remembers that it was Jesus's practice to pray in the Temple while at the same exposing the hypocrisy of its priests, MacLeod petitioned:

> *Give us grace in our changing day*
> *to stand by the temple that is the present church.*

The noisome temple
the sometime scandalized temple
that is the present church,
listening sometime to what again seems mumbo jumbo.
Make it our custom to go
till the new outline of your body for our day
becomes visible in our midst.[20]

So although he was critical of religious hypocrisy and irrelevance, MacLeod believed that the church could be redeemed to become again a blessing for the world. He was forever looking for the new outline of Christ's body, by which he meant new manifestations of Christhood in our lives and world that we have not known before, fresh acts of faithfulness to the earth and the human soul as sacred.

I first met George MacLeod in 1979. I was a young student of theology at the time and had recently heard him speak in Edinburgh. Hearing him on that first occasion had been like coming home for me. Here was a Christian teacher speaking of the sacredness of the earth and of nonviolence as essential to the way of true relationship. It was as if his words were giving voice to what my soul was longing for, even though I did not yet fully know what I was seeking.

My wife, Ali, and I were on Iona walking along the coastal path on the eastern side of the island one afternoon when we bumped into the great man. I can't remember how he greeted us, so unexpected was it to actually meet him. Ali already knew the MacLeods, as their families had been friendly over the years. But after some brief words of introduction, he said, "Newell, come back for a whiskey." I'm not sure I had ever had a whiskey before, and certainly not before 5 p.m.! But there was no thought of declining his invitation. So back we headed to Carraig Beag, the house at Martyr's Bay where MacLeod and his wife were staying.

Lorna was as formidable a character as George, a Scottish aristocrat and as conservative politically as he was socialist. They clearly loved one another, but they were like sparring partners, forever debating matters of state and society. Years earlier, he had dedicated one of his books to her, *Only One Way Left*, a title that left nothing to the imagination as far as his political leanings went. The playful dedication read, "To Lorna, who is always right"!

Ali and Lorna got to talking on one side of the room, while MacLeod and I spoke on the other. We discussed the growing environmental crisis and the movement for nuclear disarmament. And I shall always remember what he said to me at the end of that first conversation, "Newell, what are we going to do about all this?"

Two things will forever remain with me about that question,

and they are more important to me now than ever. First was his use of the word *we*. He was in his eighties. I was in my twenties. He could so easily have said, "Young man, let me tell you what to do." But part of MacLeod's greatness was that he knew the importance of the word *we* in building community and effecting real change in the world.

And the second aspect of MacLeod's question that has been with me ever since that day was his use of the word *do*. "What are we going to *do* about all this?" He was not just challenging me to think or pray or hope in new ways. Yes, all of these, but more. He was also inviting me to *do*, to speak and act, to give voice and embody vision. This for MacLeod was the way of enabling change.

"Matter matters." "Do you believe in nonviolence?" "Are you a Presbyterian or a Christian?" These were the enduring mantras of his vision. It would be difficult to imagine just how many times he repeated these words, but challenging words need to be repeated, again and again. Otherwise we are prone to forget.

In his final years a reporter asked MacLeod how it was that he had remained so single-minded in his life, to which he replied, "I've remained single-minded by being deaf." MacLeod's was a typically humorous response, but he was not deaf in his soul. Yes, he had problems with his physical hearing in later years, but his spirit remained sharply attentive to the cries of humanity and the earth. In his last days, as people visited him at the family home on Learmonth Terrace in Edinburgh, he would often simply recite the Beatitudes to them, especially, "Blessed are the peacemakers, for they will be called children of God" (Matt. 5:9).

My last conversation with George MacLeod was the year before he died. It was August 6, 1990, the feast day of the Transfiguration, when the Christian community remembers the story of Jesus glistening with light on a mountaintop, manifesting the glory of heaven in the matter of earth. It was also the forty-fifth anniversary of the dropping of the atom bomb on Hiroshima. The British newspaper *The Guardian* had asked me to write an article remembering those who had died at Hiroshima, the tens of thousands who were immediately scorched to death by the bomb as well as the countless others who later suffered and died from the effects of radiation. The words I wrote that day were quintessentially MacLeod. I spoke of light as sacred and said that at Hiroshima we took that sacredness, what he called the key to love, and used it for hell and destruction.

MacLeod read my article that day and liked it. But at the age of ninety-five he was becoming confused about certain things. So he not only liked the article; he thought he had written it. And in a sense of course it *was* his article. But he instructed his personal assistant in Edinburgh to run off hundreds of copies, so that he could send the article out to friends and contacts throughout the country. Just before it was sent, however, his daughter Mary came in and said, "Father, this isn't your article. This is Philip's article." So, man of action that he was, he picked up the phone immediately and called me on Iona.

When I say this was my last *conversation* with MacLeod, what I mean is that I think I said, "Hello." To which MacLeod replied, "Newell, MacLeod here. Such a good article, thought it was my own." Click.

MacLeod died on June 27, 1991. When word came through from Edinburgh to Iona that morning of MacLeod's death, we realized we wanted to do something immediately on the island to honor him. There would of course be the funeral and then a public memorial service on the Scottish mainland in the days and weeks to come, but on this day, the day of his death, we wanted simply to gather in the abbey church and remember him.

But first of all, we needed to get the word out. Whenever in the past I had been training new bell ringers on Iona, a procedure that would usually take at least half an hour of continuous ringing of the bell, people on the island and sometimes even from the next island over, on hearing the constant sounding of the bell, would phone up and say, "Has Lord MacLeod died?" So on the day of his death we knew we must ring the bell. We did so continuously, for an hour. And we didn't just toll the great bell of the abbey tower, we swung it, so there was an uninterrupted pealing forth of sound across the island.

By the end of the hour, the abbey church was full. Members of the community, islanders, and day visitors gathered in silence simply to hear some of MacLeod's prayers read aloud. This was the prayer I concluded with that day:

> *Be thou, triune God, in the midst of us as we give thanks for those who have gone from the sight of earthly eyes. They, in thy nearer presence, still worship with us in the mystery of the one family in heaven and on earth. . . . If it be thy holy will, tell them how we love them, and how we miss them, and how we long to be with them again.*
>
> *Strengthen us to go on in loving service of all thy children. Thus shall we have communion with thee and, in thee, with those who have gone before us. Thus shall we come to know within ourselves that there is no death and that only a veil divides, thin as gossamer.*[21]

Through the veil that is thin as gossamer, we can hear Mac-Leod and the many Celtic prophets before him asking, "What are we going to do about all this?" And with them we can keep praying, "Strengthen us, O God, to go on in loving service of all thy children."

MacLeod is an icon of compassion and justice for us today. His compassion, which was the bringing of his heart into relationship with the sacred heart of those who suffer, led to his work for justice. It was his commitment to justice that grounded his vision. It led him, as it has led great prophets of Celtic wisdom over the centuries, to seek what is just for the poorest among us, addressing the physical needs of humanity—hunger, homelessness, and ill health. It led him also, at a prophetically early stage in the modern world, to be calling for a just relationship with the earth.

Our vision of reawakening to sacredness needs to be grounded in action. It is not enough only to *see* compassionately. Nor is it enough even just to *feel* compassionately, as essential as this is. Compassion needs also to be embodied, both in the relationships of our lives and communities and in the structures of our societies and nations. Without grounding compassion justly in the detail of relationship we rob it of its greatest power to transform and heal. We are body-souls, says MacLeod, part of the body-soul of the earth. So matter matters, and justice is the absolute imperative of sacredness.

Before concluding this chapter, I invite you to take a few minutes to pay attention to what MacLeod has awakened in you. As you do the reflection practice below, sitting in silence, name in gratitude what has been stirring within you from this chapter. (All of the meditative practices are collected in the appendix, which can be used on a daily basis to remain alert to what has been calling your inner attention as you read this book.)

Reflection: Sacred Compassion

Words of Awareness

George MacLeod awakens us to the compassion of God that is deep in our souls. He prophetically calls it forth into action in our lives to serve the sacredness of humanity and the earth.

(Reflect for a brief time on the ways this wisdom applies to your life.)

Prayer of Awareness

Awake, O my soul,
To the compassion of the divine deep within you.
Awake to its sacred flow of feeling
and its strong currents for change.
Be true to it in yourself. Set it free in others.
Awake, O my soul,
To the compassion of the divine deep within you.

(Listen silently for a few minutes within the sacredness of your being.)

Awake, O my soul. Awake.

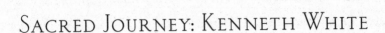

SACRED JOURNEY: KENNETH WHITE

Pilgrimage has been a pronounced feature of the Celtic world over the centuries, and it continues today. Every year thousands of men and women from all over the world travel to holy sites like Iona in Scotland or walk the ancient Camino pilgrimage route to Santiago de Compostela in Galicia. But alongside these more prominent outward journeys there is another mode of Celtic pilgrimage in which the destination is not known. This is when pilgrimage becomes peregrination, as it is called, seeking one's place of resurrection, setting sail into the unknown in search of new beginnings. This is the sacred journey that opens to us from the heart of life in every moment. This is the critical journey ahead of us as a world today, if we are to find our way forward into well-being together.

A modern Celtic prophet who passionately points to this journey in his writings is the Scottish poet Kenneth White. Born in 1936 in the Gorbals of Glasgow, which included some of the worst slums of twentieth-century Scotland, White grew up not far from where the young minister George MacLeod was pursuing his vision of a just reordering of society. Although born and bred in the west of Scotland, White has spent most of his life in France and is little known in his home country. In France, however, he has been hailed as one of the foremost English-language poets of today.

Like MacLeod and so many great Celtic teachers before him, White looks for the shining that is deep in all things. He calls it the "diamond country" at the heart of life. He sees it glistening in earth, sea, and sky:

> *. . . the sea shimmering, shimmering*
> *no art can touch it, the mind can only*
> *try to become attuned to it*
> *to become quiet . . . open . . . still . . .*
> *knowing itself in the diamond country, in*
> *the ultimate unlettered light.*[1]

White stands in a succession of Celtic prophets that includes Pelagius, Eriugena, and Teilhard, all of whom he mentions by name in his poetry. In "Little Pelagian Poem," he asks, "Was there ever / a brighter mind / a more diamond being / in all the murky history of knowledge?"[2] He sees Pelagius as the fount of an underground movement of thought that has flowed from the earliest centuries in the Celtic world. He looks for signs of a resurgence of this vision, including the ancient tradition of the *scotus vagans*, the wandering Celtic teacher, who is free from the tight bonds of established thought and religion.

To speak of the "diamond country" deep in all things, is not naive romanticism. White knows that the world is both "terrible and joyous," as he puts it.[3] There is both glory and pain, beauty and suffering in our lives and world. But deepest always is the shining, or what he sometimes calls the "loveliness":

> the loveliness is everywhere
> even
> in the ugliest
> and most hostile environment
> the loveliness is everywhere
> at the turning of a corner
> in the eyes
> and on the lips
> of a stranger
> in the emptiest areas
> where is no place for hope
> and only death
> invites the heart
> the loveliness is there
> it emerges
> incomprehensible
> inexplicable
> it rises in its own reality

and what we must learn is
how to receive it
into ours[4]

We can discern in White's writings a threefold pathway. The first is what he calls "rediscovering the earth," which is about learning to come back into true relationship with the earth. The second is what he describes as "rewording the world," that is, allowing our relationship with the earth to reshape how we see and speak and relate. The third is journeying toward a "new-found land."[5] This is when, having reestablished our relationship with the earth and allowed this relationship to reshape how we speak and act, we journey toward what we have never experienced before, a new way of being.

For White, the journey of "rediscovering the earth" began when he was studying at the University of Glasgow in the 1950s. The city became for him a paradigm of late modern civilization, which he saw as unsustainable. Glasgow, crowded and industrialized, represented modernity in its death throes. He became increasingly disillusioned with the city and with city-based culture, what he called its "reduction of spirit," where "language decays" and "earth disappears":

what I'm interested in now
are the silent fields

I feel spreading all around me
the movements of the sea
the star be-spattered sky
the relation
between a body and the universe
the nebulae and a brain[6]

This was not a total rejection of the city. Rather, it was the beginning of a more intentional search in White's life for the essential interrelationship of all things and the connection of humanity with the cosmos. It was this that increasingly beckoned him, the quest to re-establish our "primordial contact" with the earth.[7] Put people in relationship with the earth again, he says, and we will learn how to be in true contact with one another.

In the city we are no longer listening to the landscape and its music. Instead, we listen to fabricated music and political argument. "I prefer pine trees to politicians," says White.[8] Imagine if, instead of listening to political argument on the news every night, we were to spend an equal amount of time listening to a grove of pine trees or being attentive to the evening breeze whispering in the branches of a tree. There is something like music there, he says. "Maybe we can at least learn to listen again to the world. Who knows into what secrets that may lead us."[9]

White sees that we are survivors of a great catastrophe, namely, the industrialized world's separation from nature. What we need is to reestablish contact with the earth and renew our lost relationship.

It was not just in Glasgow that White experienced disconnection with the earth and himself. It was also in Paris, where he went to work on his doctorate; there he observed, "I began to feel more and more separated from myself as well as others."[10] A critical turning point, however, came in White's journey when he acquired an abandoned old farmhouse in the Ardèche, in the southeast of France. There, he says, in the essentials of "solitude, silence, wind, sun, and storm" he found connection again with himself and the world:

So I have put away the books
and I watch the last apples fall
from the frosty trees

and I have seen also
acorns stretching red shoots
into the hard soil

and the white bark of the birches
was more to me than all the pages

and what I read there
bared my heart to the winter sun
and opened my brain to the wind

and suddenly
suddenly in the midst of the winter wood
I knew I had always been there

before the books
as after the books
a winter wood

and my heart bare
and my brain open to the wind[11]

The earth, our home, our place of deepest identity, the ground from which we have come is what White is calling us back into relationship with.

Like Eriugena, the ninth-century Irish teacher, White views the natural world as a sacred text. "The sound of the wind in the treetops, the roaring of the waves, all these are sacred voices."[12] And referring to the earth as text, he says:

I open the book
and the words
fly out of the page . . .
as I listen to them [the trees and the creatures] talking . . .
I hear their phrases
twining and intertwining
like carving on a stony crypt

or like the glorified lines
of a precious manuscript[13]

Beginning at the time of the industrial revolution, our Western world forgot how to read this precious manuscript. Only now are we beginning again to consult and revere it. In almost every major discipline of thought, from the sciences to the arts, from economics to theology, we are being called by prophetic voices to rediscover the earth and to allow our relationship with her to be the guiding light of the journey toward well-being.

Just as our Western civilization was created by empire, city-based rather than nature-based, so it has been with the religion of empire. Characterized by loss of relationship with the earth, it looks for the sacred beyond the natural rather than deep within the natural. White, on the other hand, speaks of the ancient Celtic world when "moor and sea meant more than any church."[14] Remembering his experiences of religion from boyhood, he writes:

in the church I attended
around the age of nine
was that stained glass window
showing a man [the Celtic saint, Kentigern]
with a book in his hand
standing on a seashore
preaching to the gulls

I'd be gazing at the window
and forgetting the sermon . . .
eager to get back out
on to the naked shore
there to walk for hours on end . . .

trying to grasp at something
that wanted no godly name
something that took the form
of blue waves and grey rock
and that tasted of salt[15]

The shoreline, where land and sea meet, is a liminal space in the Celtic world, a portal between the known and the unknown. We are close there to the beginnings of life and to earth's primordial rhythms, tasting the sacred, knowing it with all our senses, with our body's wisdom. In that space we have one foot, as it were, in the human realm and the other in the nonhuman, the world from which we have come, the "nonhuman cosmos," he says, the "chaos cosmos," the "chaosmos."[16] It is this dialogue between human and nonhuman that we must keep alive.

And dialogue with the cosmos is exactly what we often hear in White's poetry, sometimes playfully. In "Big Moon Autumn Night," he writes:

Standing on the balcony
I was saying out loud
"I love you moon, I love you moon"

like some old Zen crazy coon[17]

White's listening to the nonhuman is often in silence, a type of meditative listening. But, as he importantly reminds us, "Meditation isn't mummification."[18] It is not a deadening of the senses. Rather, it is quick movement deep within that takes us into the diamond country, moving "into the light / that is not the sun / into the waters / that are not the sea."[19] It is about accessing "in-being," as he calls it, "fields of in-being."[20]

Meditative awareness, says White, can be wonder-filled. It is "the wonderful understanding" or "wunderstanding," as he calls it:

... taking off the clothes of the mind
and making love
to the body of reality

entering the stream ...

to be alive
to all the implications ...

touching the keys of memory ...

re-membering
getting it all together

exciting insighting[21]

Entering the stream is about accessing a subterranean flow of Light that is deep in all things. It is not just about being aware of this flow; it is about knowing the flow, and letting go to the "glow-flow" that courses through us and through the veins of the universe.[22]

As we reawaken to our relationship with the earth, we will begin to see in new ways and be prompted to live and speak in new ways. White calls this "rewording the world":

Entering this valley
is like entering a memory

. . . the feeling
of a paradise lost
about to be regained

what is this valley
that speaks to me like a memory
whispering in all its branches
this november morning? . . .

I must enter this birch-world
and speak from within it
I must enter into
this lighted silence . . .

[and wait] for the words
to come out of the silence . . .

rooted and branched
and running with sap[23]

Learning again how to speak from within our relationship with the earth has a number of significant implications. Rewording the world can lead us to be part of "reworlding the world," fashioning it anew. Or, as White says, "geo-poetics," which is how he describes a poetry that is rooted in the earth, leads to "geo-politics," which is political vision that cares for the earth.[24]

White's doctorate in Paris in the early 1960s was entitled "Poetry and Politics." He argued that a language shaped by the earth leads not only to ecological awareness, but to ecological action. By the mid-1960s he was teaching at the University of Bordeaux. These were politically turbulent times in France. Students were on the streets calling for a new social order. White supported them while also advising against strident ideologies. "Not Mao," he said, but "Tao."[25] In other words, it was not simply about attachment to political ideas, but about living in relation to the flow that is deep in the natural world.

But speaking out is essential. As White says, "seeing and saying . . . is power."[26] When we see in new ways and have the courage to speak it, we access a deep power of the soul. In the Celtic world from the earliest centuries, speech was viewed as our greatest strength, greater than any physical force. True words hold a mighty energy for change. This is truth-force or soul-force, in Gandhian terminology. It is the power of truth spoken from the heart of our being into the heart of our listeners, allowing what is deepest in us to awaken what is deepest in them. But this is not what the University of Bordeaux was looking for in its young professor, so in 1968 he was fired. The following year the University of Paris offered White a teaching post. Then in 1983 he became Professor of Modern Poetry at the Sorbonne in Paris.

Close to the heart of White's vision is the belief that we can allow our relationship with the earth to reshape how we live and speak. This includes poetic speech, which he sees as the purest expression of language. Its origins are primal; they began long before the advent of literature. Poetry, he insists, is not to be confused with versification. It is not about learning the rhythm of metrics. It is about learning the rhythm of the earth. "For a sense of rhythm," he says, "it is better to get someone to walk along the shore on a windy day than to teach him versification."[27] In other words, the universe itself is *the great* poem, and we are invited to be part of the continuing expression of this poem in how we speak and live and relate. In true poetic utterance we express ourselves with both the "intimacy" and the "immensity" of the universe.[28] The cosmos is always both intimate and immense. Its deepest energies are always closer to us than our very breath, and its vastness and interrelatedness are always greater than any of the boundaries we have placed around ourselves as nations, races, and religions.

In his poem "Full Moon and a Wind from the North," White writes:

> *up at four*
> *walking along*
> *a silent shore*
>
> *trying to translate*
> *into a tongue that's known*
> *a poem writ*
> *in the language of stone*[29]

The poetry is already there, deep in the matter of the earth, even in its geological formations. It is in the stuff and interrelationship of the universe. Our role is to translate it into human speech and action, both individually and collectively.

White reminds us that poetry is often rough and unfinished— like the universe. It is not always sweet and pretty. As he writes in "Crow Meditation":

Everybody knows
the sad sweet tale
of the nightingale
but when crow starts croaking
hard and hoarse
that's something else

crow, I tell you, is one queer joe

crow is a ghost
he's a bird with a past

crow is king
of his own mad world
in which he's always croaking

usually
nobody listens to crow

but when one of your friends
takes off for the icelands
and writes back in a letter
about a weird crow-encounter
somewhere in the snowfields
and when a few days later
as you come through the door

of a Montparnasse apartment
the first thing you set eyes on
is a huge lump of crow
whose croaking days are over
but looks as if it knew
a thing or two

you begin to wonder
you find yourself asking
what there is to crow

why does crow crow?
where does crow go?
what does crow know?
. . .

all birds
talk dawn-talk
in different lingos[30]

"Dawn-talk," the language that emerges from the meeting of day and night. Twilight, as we have seen, is sacred in the Celtic world. It is the time governed neither by the sun nor by the moon but by the meeting of the two, the intertwining of night and day, known and unknown, conscious and unconscious. It is a time loved especially by the birds who give voice to it in their "different lingos," whether harsh or sweet, loud or soft, calling our attention to the liminal world and the meeting of so-called opposites. "I have studied the language of dawn", says White.[31] It is free from the dualisms of sun and moon, darkness and light, dreaming and waking. By learning this language, he says, maybe we can move beyond the fixed categories of opposites that have dominated our Western world, of seen and unseen, spirit and matter, "maybe a space in which these notions . . . are no longer contradictory."[32]

Because White rejects dualism, he hesitates to use the word "God." For him it belongs to the old dualistic order that has done such "harm," as he says, separating spirit from matter, the transcendent from the immanent, heaven from earth.[33] I understand his hesitancy. Maybe we need a moratorium on the word for some time, to free us from the harmful ways in which it has been used to divide rather than unite. But, in the end, I believe we need this word because, as the great Jewish teacher Martin Buber said, it is a primordial word. It comes from the earliest strands of human consciousness, deep in the unfolding history of the human mystery, earlier than the recorded beginnings of religion and culture. So if we are to integrate our past with the future and the essence of our spiritual inheritance with the unfolding path ahead of us, this word, if redeemed, can be part of the way forward, part of our healing and reintegration. But we will see.

Rediscovering the earth and rewording the world will lead us on a journey toward what we have never experienced before, toward a "new-found land," says White, a way of being in relationship with the earth and one another that is radically new. White uses Jacques Cartier, the sixteenth-century French Celt who sailed the Atlantic in search of a passage to the East, as a metaphor for this journeying through the unknown. "I suppose what I'm after," he says, is "a kind of cartography."[34] It is like mapping our way forward, navigating into a new way of being.

He describes the journey essentially as pilgrimage, indeed as "peregrination," a search for one's place of resurrection, of radically new beginnings.[35] And it is resurrection that we are in need of, not simply resuscitation. As psychologist Carl Jung says of the Christian Easter myth, the risen Christ is not found where his body was laid. It is not simply the old in reanimated form. It is something that exceeds what has been experienced and even imagined.

The key literary figure in White's journey motif is St. Brendan of Clonfert (although White prefers to call him Brandan). This sixth-century Irish saint is often referred to historically as Brendan the Navigator or Brendan the Voyager, with reference to his legendary sailing of the Atlantic in search of the Garden of Eden. Some historians argue that he may have been the first to cross the Atlantic, long before the Vikings or Christopher Columbus reached North America. For White, Brandan is a symbol

of the wanderer, searching for what is beyond the horizons of the
known:

> *It was a stony kingdom*
> *on the West coast of Ireland*
> *with the wind wailing*
> *and the roaring of Atlantic breakers*
> *with strange men wandering and murmuring:*
> is e mo drui Crist mac De
> *"my druid is Christ the son of God"*
>
> *One had always wished to wander farther*
> *Brandan by name and a name it was*
> *that had the sea in it,*
> *the breaking of waves and the memory of a poem . . .*
>
> *Brandan built him[self] a boat . . .*
> *making first a framework of pliant wood*
> *covering it with bull hides tanned in oak*
> *smearing the hides with grease and resin—*
> *a boat light as a bird to ride the sea!*
>
> *when the boat was ready, firm and true*
> *he gathered men about him, saying:*
> *"this will be no pleasure cruise*
> *rather the wildest of wild goose chases*

around the rim of the world and farther
a peregrination in the name of God . . ."

They pulled away from Ireland, heading North
oars dipping into blue water
amid a caterwauling of gulls

the going was good and the rhythm sure . . .
but so far North he'd never come
the world here was at an end
here there was only sea and wind
. . .
Ah, it was beautiful, the northern blue
and the clear white curling of the surf!
every mile was a broad blue page of vellum
and Brandan was working out the words . . .
trying for a freshness never found before

Brandan the voyager would be Brandan the poet
only if he could write a poem
brighter and stronger than all other poems
a poem full of the rough sea and the light

oh, the words for it, the words for a dawning!
Farther and farther they pulled away
into the white unknown[36]

This is a journey into the unknown, says White, leaving the familiar to travel through uncharted territory in the hope of finding the new, a peregrination in the name of God. "Faith is the assurance of things hoped for, the conviction of things not seen," say the scriptures (Heb. 11:1). The journey is about opening to the way forward, trusting in what we do not yet see.

There are many journey poems in White's writings, and Brandan is not always the navigator. Sometimes the navigator remains unnamed, for the navigator in a sense is always each one of us. We are all needed on this journey, exploring the way forward together. The journey itself can be liberating, quite apart from whether or not we reach the new land:

Another dawn
out from Greenland
whales bellowing in the icy sea
and the vast sky
resounding with wind

once more I felt that breadth of mind
like being drunk
but this was colder and more clear
than anything
that might come out of a jug
it was what I'd always lived for
what I always will live for[37]

The journey itself is sacred. We may not know whether we will reach the newfound land. We may not know exactly where the journey will take us. We *can* know, however, that in opening to the journey we feel more alive, more true. In opening to the journey together we can be part of nurturing hope in one another, even though at times it will feel more like "hoping against hope" (Rom. 4:18), hoping against all the odds of reaching a new land.

In one of White's journey poems entitled "Labrador" the voyager indeed reaches what he calls "a new land." But still he needs to keep moving "step by step" farther and farther into the reality. Labrador, which adjoins Newfoundland, becomes a metaphor of being on the edge, as it were, of the newfound land. But still there is the need to feel the way forward:

> *I was aware of a new land*
> *a new world*
> *but I was loath to name it too soon*
> *simply content to use my senses*
> *feeling my way*
> *step by step into the reality . . .*
>
> *I lived and moved*
> *as I had never done before . . .*
> *knew a larger identity*

the tracks of caribou in the snow
the flying of wild geese
the red Autumn of the maple tree
bitten by frost
all these became more real to me
more really me
than my very name

I found myself still saying things like
"at one with the spirit of the land"
but there was no "spirit," none
that was outworn language
and this was a new world
and my mind was, almost, a new mind
there was no such thing as "spirit"
only the blue tracks in the snow
the flying of the geese
the frost-bitten leaf

religion and philosophy
what I'd learned in the churches and the schools
were all too heavy
for this travelling life
all that remained to me was poetry
but a poetry

as unobtrusive as breathing
a poetry like the wind
and the maple leaf
that I spoke to myself
moving over the land[38]

We are on the edge of the new. We are sensing a different way of journeying with the earth and one another. We are being guided by a conviction of things not yet seen, a faith in what we can only hope for. Maybe we are beginning to imagine what it might look like, although White cautions us from naming it too soon or trying to define it too sharply with terminology from our old, worn categories of thought and perception, like spirit and matter. Rather, we are to simply continue feeling our way farther forward, step by step.

White's voyagers never try to conquer or name the new land they are entering. Nor do they try to tame or Christianize it. They simply journey farther into it and open themselves to it more and more:

Brandan was maybe a believer
but that's neither here nor there
first and foremost
he was a navigator
a figure moving mile by mile
along the headlands
among the islands

tracing a way
between foam and cloud
with an eye to outlines . . .

and a world
opening, opening![39]

White is inviting us to open our minds and imaginations to what we have not yet experienced, navigating together a way forward for the world in a journey that is forever opening, opening.

Kenneth White is a Celtic prophet, and, like all prophets, he is not perfect. He does not provide all the answers, and his words can be challenging to live with. For many of us he may not provide enough creative tension with the old, he may too readily have sacrificed a sense of transcendence, and he may not sufficiently offer a vision of community. But he is part of glimpsing the way forward. His call to rediscover the earth, to reword the world, and to journey toward a newfound land speaks to us faithfully from the heart of this moment in time.

We are, as one of his voyagers says, "halfway between the Old World and the New," and it is becoming clearer and clearer that we as a modern world did not set sail soon enough on this journey of coming back into relationship with the earth.[40] The repercussions will be severe, for both the earth and the human community. The repercussions are already severe. But the possibility of journeying is still open to us, and it can be a sacred journey regardless of when we have started or how great the challenges are. In a sense we are always between the old and the new, the known and the unknown, halfway between what has been and what is trying to become. In every moment, in every journey and challenge we can be looking for new dawnings. Within ourselves and in the most intimate relationships of our lives, we can be waiting with expectancy for what we have not even dared imagine. Waiting, alert, and open to the journey.

And so White calls out to the creatures above us who announce the dawning of each day, to the birds of the air who know dawn-talk, and especially to the wild geese, who in the Celtic world are harbingers of spring, messengers of resurrection:

> *please keep on using the sky*
> *as you know how*
> *riding the wind*
> *with your eyes wide open*
> *tracing out the shoreline*
> *(along with something else it's harder to define)*
> *and throw out a cry or two now and then*
> *for those of us down here who care*
> *that'll be a kind of reminder*

(to accompany the signs
we read silent in the stone):
way beyond the heart's house
right into the bone[41]

Brandan and the many voyagers of vision who have journeyed before us show us how to sail with faith, letting go of the old in search of the new, our eyes wide open for the shoreline of a land we have not yet entered. "Dawn comes," writes White, "with the cry of the wild goose."[42]

White is an icon for us today of the voyager, the one who has set sail to discover a new land, a new way of being. He let go of the old order and sought the new. Early on in his life he realized that our city-based culture, born of the industrial revolution, is bankrupt and unsustainable. He began instead to seek an earth-based orientation for his life and journey. The same was true for him in the fields of poetry, politics, and philosophy—he believed that we are to navigate forward into new ways of seeing based on our primal relationship with the earth. White is a mapmaker, charting the way into new territory.

Many of us today in the Western world are aware that the old order is not working—politically, socially, environmentally, religiously. Countless numbers of us from the Christian community have already lifted anchor and are sailing out of the harbor of our religious homeland, even though we may not know where we are heading or how far we need to go. The good news is that we do not need to know exactly where we are heading. We can choose to be part of an ancient spiritual practice of peregrination, leaving home or the comfort of the familiar in order to seek resurrection, new beginnings.

This is not simply a passive drifting into new waters. It can be a faith-filled letting go of what is no longer working in order to travel with an inner assurance toward what we are longing for, our eyes open, skinned for the shoreline of "a better country" (Heb. 11:16). Each one of us is a voyager. This is what the universe invites us to be in our lives and relationships, because the universe keeps changing, unfolding, evolving. Anything that resists new beginnings and new ways is finished. The invitation is to voyage faithfully, alert even in dark times for the glimmerings of fresh light. Always we can be alert to the cry of the wild goose and the coming of a new dawn.

Before concluding this chapter, I invite you to take a few minutes to pay attention to what White has awakened in you. As you do the reflection practice below, sitting in silence, name in gratitude what has been stirring within you from this chapter. (All of the meditative practices are collected in the appendix, which can be used on a daily basis to remain alert to what has been calling your inner attention as you read this book.)

REFLECTION: SACRED JOURNEY

WORDS OF AWARENESS

Kenneth White invites us into a journey of opening to new ways of seeing and being. It is a journey that will take us through unknown waters, sometimes troubled, sometimes clear, into a new relationship with the earth. It is a journey of faith, a peregrination in the name of God.

(Reflect for a brief time on the ways this wisdom applies to your life.)

PRAYER OF AWARENESS

Awake, O my soul,
To the prayer of dawn that is within you.
Listen to its hopes for a new day.
Follow its intimations of fresh light.
You are an explorer of what has never been before.
Awake, O my soul,
To the prayer of dawn that is within you.

(Listen silently for a few minutes within the sacredness of your being.)

Awake, O my soul. Awake.

CONCLUSION

A few years ago, halfway through a talk I was delivering in California on some of the themes of this book, a woman in the audience, who in fact had attended many of my talks before, leaned toward the person sitting next to her and, intending to whisper, ended up saying in a voice that could be heard by nearly everyone in the room, "He's a f—ing radical."

This, I should say, was not intended to be a criticism. It was an endorsement! Isn't it interesting, though, that she had only just realized this. She had heard me speak many times before. But suddenly it all connected. She had put two and two together. She saw that to speak of the sacredness of the earth and the sacredness of every human being holds enormous implications for us today, in fact radical implications for how we are to live and relate to one another and the earth.

After the talk, realizing that her attempt at a whisper had in fact been a stage whisper, she apologized for her colorful comment. I thanked her for the apology but said I didn't require one, not at all. I was delighted that she had seen the implications. This is precisely why we need to hear again these great prophetic voices from the Celtic world. They help reawaken us to the sacred in ways that profoundly challenge how we live.

This is why Pelagius was banished from the empire, why legends about Brigid were toned down by medieval Catholicism, and why Eriugena was condemned by Rome. This is why the people of the *Carmina Gadelica* were persecuted by religious and political authorities in Scotland, and why Alexander John Scott was deposed from the ministry. It is the same reason John Muir's attempts to save Hetch Hetchy Valley in Yosemite were defeated by Congress. Similarly, it is why Teilhard was forbidden by the Vatican to teach, why the BBC silenced MacLeod during the war, and why the University of Bordeaux fired Kenneth White. When the prophet is allowed to speak, the people begin to remember what they deeply know, that the earth and all things are sacred. And this memory holds urgent implications for how we are to care for the well-being and dignity of all people and for the health and sustainability of the earth.

Other prophets could be added to this stream of wisdom that comes down to us over the centuries in the Celtic world. The voice of one of these is being heard today as it never was during her own lifetime. I speak of the Scottish poet and writer Nan Shepherd (1893–1981). She is gaining our attention, certainly in Scotland, so much so that she now appears on the Scottish five-pound note, honored as a woman of the imagination with a passion for the earth. She is the female equivalent of John Muir, giving voice to the sacred interrelationship of all things.[1]

The prophetic vision of figures like Muir and Shepherd is gaining more and more currency among us today. We are in the midst of a great reawakening to the sacredness of the earth and the human soul. Yes, there is also reaction to this awakening on the part of those who have vested interest in maintaining systems that neglect the sacredness of every species and that deny the sacredness of every race, gender, and sexual orientation. But these reactionary forces do not represent the deep spirit of this moment in time. Rather, they represent a frightened denial of this awakening. This is not to downplay their power and the might of their resistance. Nor is it to underestimate the enormous task ahead of us in confronting and challenging systems of inequity and neglect. But the deep momentum of this present moment is toward a greater consciousness of the sacred in all things.

There is a groundswell of waking up to the dignity of every human being and every race. There is a reawakened awareness of the sacred feminine. There is a sharpened scientific understanding of the single flow of life that courses through the body of the universe. There is a rediscovery of the power of native song and story to help inspire our rituals and narratives of sacredness today. There is a new openness to the intuitive and the imaginative as essential tools in discerning the way forward in our lives and world.

There is an explosion of earth awareness in our human consciousness, the likes of which we have never known before. There is an awakened sensitivity to how we handle matter and the stuff of the earth. There is a growing mindfulness of compassion and how to embody it in our lives and relationships. And there is an ever-awakening realization that humanity must journey forward into a new reverence for the earth, if the world as we know it is to survive.

Sacred Earth, Sacred Soul is a reflection of this groundswell of awakening. I offer this book in the hope that it will further deepen and strengthen the awakenings that we are in the midst of now. To know that there has been a continuous stream of Celtic wisdom running through the centuries that we can draw on for today is a great resource for the journey ahead. We do not have to invent a new way of seeing. This is a wisdom tradition that has evolved and unfolded in the Celtic world over many centuries. Our role is simply to apply it in new ways for today. It is a stream of wisdom that nourishes the deepest knowing of our being, that the earth and every human being is sacred.

On the Scottish five-pound note, beside the image of Nan Shepherd, is a quotation from one of her novels: "It's a grand thing to get leave to live." It is a great thing to have been given opportunity to live, an almost unbelievable gift. The rising of the sun each day, our very breath, the birth of our children, our capacity to sense and dream and imagine—these are all pure grace.

A major feature of the wisdom tradition we have been drawing on in these pages is gratitude. Remembering that what shines most deeply in the face of a newborn child is sacredness and that this sacredness, deep within each of us, infuses every creature and life-form lead to a deep posture of gratitude. Gratefulness for the sacredness of one another and the earth, including gratitude for the gifts of sight and sound, of touch and taste and scent that we may know one another and the body of the earth, is what we are being invited to reawaken to. It will change the way we live and relate and act.

And if I may build on Shepherd's words to make my final point, I would say, it is a grand thing to get leave to love. It is utterly grand. Or, as the woman in California who woke up halfway through my talk might put it, radically grand! For love, like nothing else, is the fire that fully reawakens us to the sacred in one another and the earth. In the Celtic world reawakening to the sacred is reawakening to love. The two are inseparably intertwined.

This is the call for us today. From Pelagius and Brigid of Kildare to today, Celtic prophets are calling us to wake up to what is deepest in all things, the sacredness of the divine, and to remember that deep within this sacredness is love. This is the love that we can offer one another and the earth. This is the love that we can receive from one another and the earth. When we love, we are most truly alive. When we love, we are most fully awake to the true heart of the other, made of God, sacred.

Appendix: A Nine-Day Cycle of Meditative Awareness

Day One: Sacred Soul

Words of Awareness

You have been graced with the dignity of divine birth, says Pelagius. Live this dignity in your life, safeguard it in one another, and protect it in every human being.

(Reflect for a brief time on the ways this wisdom applies to your life.)

Prayer of Awareness

Awake, O my soul,
And know the sacred dignity of your being.
Awake to it in every living soul this day.
Honor it, defend it,
In heart and mind, in word and deed.
Awake, O my soul,
And know the sacred dignity of your being.

(Listen silently for a few minutes within the sacredness of your being.)

Awake, O my soul. Awake.

Day Two: Sacred Feminine

Words of Awareness

St. Brigid embodies the beauty and strength of the sacred feminine, which is deep within us all. Stories of her life call forth this dimension of the divine in us, that we may be strong again to serve the interrelationship of all things, within us, between us, and among us in the world.

(Reflect for a brief time on the ways this wisdom applies to your life.)

Prayer of Awareness

Awake, O my soul,
To the beauty of the divine deep within you
And awake to its fragrance in the body of the earth.
Know its strength of attraction
And its grace to heal what has been torn apart.
Awake, O my soul,
To the beauty of the divine deep within you.

(Listen silently for a few minutes within the sacredness of your being.)

Awake, O my soul. Awake.

Day Three: Sacred Flow

Words of Awareness

John Scotus Eriugena sees the divine as a subterranean river flowing through the body of the earth and through everything that has being. This sacred river runs also through you and through me. We can open to it now to be more fully alive.

(Reflect for a brief time on the ways this wisdom applies to your life.)

Prayer of Awareness

Awake, O my soul,
To the flow of the divine deep within you.
Awake to it in every creature, in every woman, in every man.
It is our river of resurrection, the promise of new beginnings.
Awake, O my soul,
To the flow of the divine deep within you.

(Listen silently for a few minutes within the sacredness of your being.)

Awake, O my soul. Awake.

Day Four: Sacred Song

Words of Awareness

The people of the *Carmina Gadelica* carried within themselves a song of the earth and the human soul. It is a song of strength and vision that we can choose to sing in new ways today.

(*Reflect for a brief time on the ways this wisdom applies to your life.*)

Prayer of Awareness

Awake, O my soul,
To the ever new song of the earth that is within you.
Awake to its rhythms and seasons,
Its memories of joy and lament
And its eternal hopes of fresh buddings and births.
Awake, O my soul,
To the ever new song of the earth that is within you.

(*Listen silently for a few minutes within the sacredness of your being.*)

Awake, O my soul. Awake.

Day Five: Sacred Imagination

Words of Awareness

Alexander John Scott taught that in every moment and encounter of life we can imagine the intermingling of heaven and earth, time and eternity, spirit and matter. Together we can dream our way forward into what has never been before.

(*Reflect for a brief time on the ways this wisdom applies to your life.*)

Prayer of Awareness

Awake, O my soul,
To the sacred dreams that are stirring within you.
Awake to the imaginations of the heart
And the cherished hopes of what is yet to be.
Do not be afraid.
Awake, O my soul.
To the sacred dreams that are stirring within you.

(*Listen silently for a few minutes within the sacredness of your being.*)

Awake, O my soul. Awake.

Day Six: Sacred Earth

Words of Awareness

John Muir says that deep within the human soul is a primal love of the earth. We don't have to create or manufacture this love. Our role is simply to awaken to it again and release it in one another, so that together we may serve the earth with passion.

(Reflect for a brief time on the ways this wisdom applies to your life.)

Prayer of Awareness

Awake, O my soul,
And know that you are born of the earth.
Awake to your love for her,
Sown like a seed in the womb of your beginnings.
Honor her, protect her, cherish and adore her.
Awake, O my soul,
And know that you are born of the earth.

(Listen silently for a few minutes within the sacredness of your being.)

Awake, O my soul. Awake.

DAY SEVEN: SACRED MATTER

WORDS OF AWARENESS

Pierre Teilhard de Chardin awakens us to the sacredness of matter. The body of the earth, including the human body, has a translucence through which the Light of the divine can be glimpsed. At the heart of matter is the heart of God.

(Reflect for a brief time on the ways this wisdom applies to your life.)

PRAYER OF AWARENESS

Awake, O my soul,
To the sacred stream of light that runs through you.
Awake to it in the body of the earth and every life-form,
In the moist fecundity of valleys
And the hard matter of mountain granite,
All things in flux and further becoming.
Awake, O my soul,
To the sacred stream of light that runs through you.

(Listen silently for a few minutes within the sacredness of your being.)

Awake, O my soul. Awake.

DAY EIGHT: SACRED COMPASSION

WORDS OF AWARENESS

George MacLeod awakens us to the compassion of God that is deep in our souls. He prophetically calls it forth into action in our lives to serve the sacredness of humanity and the earth.

(Reflect for a brief time on the ways this wisdom applies to your life.)

PRAYER OF AWARENESS

Awake, O my soul,
To the compassion of the divine deep within you.
Awake to its sacred flow of feeling
and its strong currents for change.
Be true to it in yourself. Set it free in others.
Awake, O my soul,
To the compassion of the divine deep within you.

(Listen silently for a few minutes within the sacredness of your being.)

Awake, O my soul. Awake.

Day Nine: Sacred Journey

Words of Awareness

Kenneth White invites us into a journey of opening to new ways of seeing and being. It is a journey that will take us through unknown waters, sometimes troubled, sometimes clear, into a new relationship with the earth. It is a journey of faith, a peregrination in the name of God.

(Reflect for a brief time on the ways this wisdom applies to your life.)

Prayer of Awareness

Awake, O my soul,
To the prayer of dawn that is within you.
Listen to its hopes for a new day.
Follow its intimations of fresh light.
You are an explorer of what has never been before.
Awake, O my soul,
To the prayer of dawn that is within you.

(Listen silently for a few minutes within the sacredness of your being.)

Awake, O my soul. Awake.

NOTES

CHAPTER 1: SACRED SOUL: PELAGIUS

1. Robert M. Grant, *Irenaeus of Lyons* (London: Routledge, 1997), 136.

2. Grant, *Irenaeus of Lyons*, 150

3. Grant, *Irenaeus of Lyons*, 167, 169.

4. James P. MacKey, ed., *An Introduction to Celtic Christianity* (Edinburgh: Clark, 1989), 388.

5. MacKey, ed., *Introduction to Celtic Christianity*, 389.

6. B. R. Rees, ed., *The Letters of Pelagius and His Followers* (Woodbridge: Boydell, 1991), 37.

7. MacKey, ed., *Introduction to Celtic Christianity*, 391.

8. Robert Van de Weyer, ed., *The Letters of Pelagius* (Evesham: Arthur James, 1995), 46.

9. Rees, ed., *Letters of Pelagius and His Followers*, 54.

10. Rees, ed., *Letters of Pelagius and His Followers*, 39.

11. See the treatment of Pelagius in G. de Plinval, *Pélage* (Lausanne: Payot, 1943).

12. Van de Weyer, ed., *Letters of Pelagius*, 36.

13. Van de Weyer, ed., *Letters of Pelagius*, 71.

14. Rees, ed., *Letters of Pelagius and His Followers*, 67.

15. Van de Weyer, ed., *Letters of Pelagius*, 58.

16. Van de Weyer, ed., *Letters of Pelagius*, 66.

17. Rees, ed., *Letters of Pelagius and His Followers*, 43.

18. Rees, ed., *Letters of Pelagius and His Followers*, 124.

19. Van de Weyer, ed., *Letters of Pelagius*, 72.

20. Rees, ed., *Letters of Pelagius and His Followers*, 183.

21. Bede, *Ecclesiastical History of the English People* (London: Penguin, 1990), 139.

22. Rees, ed., *Letters of Pelagius and His Followers*, 84.

CHAPTER 2: SACRED FEMININE: ST. BRIGID OF KILDARE

1. Alexander Carmichael, ed., *Carmina Gadelica* (Edinburgh: Floris, 1994), 580–81.

2. Carmichael, ed., *Carmina Gadelica*, 297.

3. Brian Wright, *Brigid: Goddess, Druidess and Saint* (Stroud: History Press, 2014), 40.

4. Wright, *Brigid*, 81.

5. Carmichael, ed., *Carmina Gadelica*, 581.

6. Carmichael, ed., *Carmina Gadelica*, 299.

7. Carmichael, ed., *Carmina Gadelica*, 56.

8. John Philip Newell, ed., *The Iona Community Worship Book* (Glasgow: Wild Goose, 1988), 27.

9. O. Davies, ed., "The Irish Life of Brigit," *Celtic Spirituality* (Mahwah: Paulist Press, 1999), 143.

10. "The Irish Life of Brigit," 138.

11. "The Irish Life of Brigit," 147.

12. Wright, *Brigid*, 157.

13. Courtney Weber, *Brigid: History, Mystery, and Magick of the Celtic Goddess* (San Francisco: Weiser, 2015), 147.

14. Carmichael, ed., *Carmina Gadelica*, 367.

15. Carmichael, ed., *Carmina Gadelica*, 344.

16. Wright, *Brigid*, 89.

17. Wright, *Brigid*, 189.

CHAPTER 3: SACRED FLOW: JOHN SCOTUS ERIUGENA

1. *The Church Hymnary*, 3rd ed. (London: Oxford Univ. Press, 1973), 577.

2. Bede, *Ecclesiastical History of the English People* (London: Penguin, 1990), 106.

3. Arthur W. Haddan and William Stubbs, eds., *Councils and Ecclesiastical Documents Relating to Great Britain and Ireland, vol. 2, part 1* (Oxford: Oxford Univ. Press, 1873), 121.

4. Bede, *Ecclesiastical History*, 82–88.
5. Bede, *Ecclesiastical History*, 188–92.
6. Nora Chadwick, *The Celts* (London: Penguin, 1971), 206.
7. John T. McNeill, *The Celtic Churches* (Chicago: Univ. of Chicago Press, 1974), 180.
8. John Scotus Eriugena, *Periphyseon* (Montreal: Bellarmin, 1987), 116.
9. Eriugena, *Periphyseon*, 31.
10. John Scotus Eriugena, *The Voice of the Eagle* (New York: Lindisfarne, 1990), 55.
11. Eriugena, *Periphyseon*, 308.
12. Eriugena, *Voice of the Eagle,* 50.
13. Eriugena, *Periphyseon*, 593, 692.
14. Eriugena, *Periphyseon*, 482, 131.
15. Eriugena, *Periphyseon*, 536.
16. Eriugena, *Periphyseon*, 112.
17. Eriugena, *Voice of the Eagle*, 41.
18. Eriugena, *Voice of the Eagle*, 9; J. F. Kenney, *The Sources for the Early History of Ireland* (New York: Columbia Univ. Press, 1929), 578.
19. "John Scotus Eriugena," *Wikipedia*, https://en.wikipedia.org/wiki/John_Scotus_Eriugena.
20. According to the Pew Research Center on Religion and Public Life, www.pewforum.org.

CHAPTER 4: SACRED SONG: THE CARMINA GADELICA

1. Alexander Carmichael, *Carmina Gadelica: Hymns and Incantations* (Edinburgh: Floris, 1992), 260.
2. Carmichael, *Carmina Gadelica*, 204–5.
3. Carmichael, *Carmina Gadelica*, 45.
4. Carmichael, *Carmina Gadelica*, 630.
5. Carmichael, *Carmina Gadelica*, 286.
6. Carmichael, *Carmina Gadelica*, 291–92.
7. Carmichael, *Carmina Gadelica*, 575.
8. Carmichael, *Carmina Gadelica*, 621.
9. Carmichael, *Carmina Gadelica*, 223–24.
10. Carmichael, *Carmina Gadelica*, 189–92.

11. Carmichael, *Carmina Gadelica*, 280.

12. John Philip Newell, ed., *The Iona Community Worship Book* (Glasgow: Wild Goose, 1988), 27.

13. Carmichael, *Carmina Gadelica*, 301.

14. Kenneth H. Jackson, ed., *A Celtic Miscellany* (London: Penguin, 1971), 109.

15. Carmichael, *Carmina Gadelica*, 253.

16. Carmichael, *Carmina Gadelica*, 312–13.

17. Carmichael, *Carmina Gadelica*, 24.

18. Carmichael, *Carmina Gadelica*, 27–28.

19. Carmichael, *Carmina Gadelica*, 24.

20. "The Clearances," *The Scotsman*, Edinburgh, February 14, 2005.

21. See Priscilla Scott, "A Sense of Place in the Poetry of Mairi Mhor Nan Oran," *The Bottle Imp*, iss. 21, June 2017, www.thebottleimp.org.uk/2017/06/a-sense-of-place -in-the-poetry-of-mairi-mhor-nan-oran.

22. Carmichael, *Carmina Gadelica*, 632.

23. Carmichael, *Carmina Gadelica*, 296, 287.

24. Scott, "A Sense of Place in the Poetry of Mairi Mhor Nan Oran."

25. Carmichael, *Carmina Gadelica*, 632.

26. Scott, "A Sense of Place in the Poetry of Mairi Mhor Nan Oran."

27. William Sharp, *The Dominion of Dreams: Under the Dark Star* (New York: Duffield, 1911), 423.

CHAPTER 5: SACRED IMAGINATION: ALEXANDER JOHN SCOTT

1. *Westminster Confession of Faith*, chap. 6, secs. 2, 4.

2. John Philip Newell, "A. J. Scott and His Circle" (PhD thesis, University of Edinburgh, 1981), 280.

3. Newell, "A. J. Scott and His Circle," 207.

4. Newell, "A. J. Scott and His Circle," 228.

5. Newell, "A. J. Scott and His Circle," 207.

6. Newell, "A. J. Scott and His Circle," 128.

7. Newell, "A. J. Scott and His Circle," 140.

8. Newell, "A. J. Scott and His Circle," 141.

9. Newell, "A. J. Scott and His Circle," 142.

10. Newell, "A. J. Scott and His Circle," 204.
11. Newell, "A. J. Scott and His Circle," 251.
12. Newell, "A. J. Scott and His Circle," 386.
13. Newell, "A. J. Scott and His Circle," 229.
14. Newell, "A. J. Scott and His Circle," 203.
15. Newell, "A. J. Scott and His Circle," 203, 254.
16. Newell, "A. J. Scott and His Circle," 346.
17. Newell, "A. J. Scott and His Circle," 433.
18. Newell, "A. J. Scott and His Circle," 234.
19. Newell, "A. J. Scott and His Circle," 248.
20. Newell, "A. J. Scott and His Circle," 249.
21. Newell, "A. J. Scott and His Circle," 233.
22. Newell, "A. J. Scott and His Circle," 281.
23. Newell, "A. J. Scott and His Circle," 361.
24. Newell, "A. J. Scott and His Circle," 326.
25. Newell, "A. J. Scott and His Circle," 340.
26. Newell, "A. J. Scott and His Circle," 362.
27. Newell, "A. J. Scott and His Circle," 355.
28. Newell, "A. J. Scott and His Circle," 279.
29. Newell, "A. J. Scott and His Circle," 296.
30. Newell, "A. J. Scott and His Circle," 305.
31. Newell, "A. J. Scott and His Circle," 404.
32. Newell, "A. J. Scott and His Circle," 143.
33. Newell, "A. J. Scott and His Circle," 251.

CHAPTER 6: SACRED EARTH: JOHN MUIR

1. Stephen K. Hatch, ed., *The Contemplative John Muir: Spiritual Quotations from the Great American Naturalist* (Boulder: Lulu.com, 2012), 173, 175.
2. Hatch, ed., *Contemplative John Muir*, 20.
3. John Muir, *Nature Writings* (New York: Library of America, 1997), 7.
4. Tim Flinders, ed., *John Muir: Spiritual Writings* (Maryknoll, NY: Orbis Books, 2013), 96.
5. Hatch, ed., *Contemplative John Muir*, 75.

6. Hatch, ed., *Contemplative John Muir*, 58, 75.
7. Flinders, ed., *John Muir*, 97.
8. Mary Colwell, *John Muir: The Scotsman Who Saved America's Wild Places* (Oxford: Lion Hudson, 2014), 82.
9. Hatch, ed., *Contemplative John Muir*, 21.
10. Flinders, ed., *John Muir*, 98.
11. Flinders, ed., *John Muir*, 66.
12. Flinders, ed., *John Muir*, 29.
13. Hatch, ed., *Contemplative John Muir*, 67.
14. Flinders, ed., *John Muir*, 100.
15. Flinders, ed., *John Muir*, 89.
16. Hatch, ed., *Contemplative John Muir*, 50.
17. Hatch, ed., *Contemplative John Muir*, 161.
18. Flinders, ed., *John Muir*, 2.
19. Flinders, ed., *John Muir*, 46
20. Flinders, ed., *John Muir*, 46.
21. Flinders, ed., *John Muir*, 91.
22. Hatch, ed., *Contemplative John Muir*, 33.
23. Flinders, ed., *John Muir*, 84.
24. Flinders, ed., *John Muir*, 52.
25. Hatch, ed., *Contemplative John Muir*, 30.
26. Flinders, ed., *John Muir*, 91.
27. Hatch, ed., *Contemplative John Muir*, 141.
28. Flinders, ed., *John Muir*, 77.
29. Flinders, ed., *John Muir*, 82–83.
30. Flinders, ed., *John Muir*, 105.
31. Hatch, ed., *Contemplative John Muir*, 207.
32. Muir, *Nature Writings*, 274, 186.
33. Colwell, *John Muir*, 207.
34. Hatch, ed., *Contemplative John Muir*, 199.
35. Flinders, ed., *John Muir*, 86–87.
36. Hatch, ed., *Contemplative John Muir*, 123–24.
37. Flinders, ed., *John Muir*, 74.
38. Hatch, ed., *Contemplative John Muir*, 290.

39. Flinders, ed., *John Muir*, 91.
40. Hatch, ed., *Contemplative John Muir*, 298.
41. Flinders, ed., *John Muir*, 95.
42. Hatch, ed., *Contemplative John Muir*, 101.
43. Hatch, ed., *Contemplative John Muir*, 96.
44. Flinders, ed., *John Muir*, 69.
45. Colwell, *John Muir*, 174.
46. Hatch, ed., *Contemplative John Muir*, 280.
47. Colwell, *John Muir*, 231.
48. Hatch, ed., *Contemplative John Muir*, 187
49. Hatch, ed., *Contemplative John Muir*, 34.
50. Flinders, ed., *John Muir*, 105.
51. "John Muir," *Wikipedia*, https://en.wikipedia.org/wiki/John_Muir.
52. Flinders, ed., *John Muir*, 96.
53. "John Muir," *Wikipedia*.

CHAPTER 7: SACRED MATTER: PIERRE TEILHARD DE CHARDIN

1. Pierre Teilhard de Chardin, *The Heart of Matter* (London: Collins, 1978), 15.
2. Pierre Teilhard de Chardin, *Le Milieu Divin* (London: Collins, 1967), 115.
3. Teilhard de Chardin, *Milieu Divin*, 78.
4. Teilhard de Chardin, *Heart of Matter*, 26.
5. Teilhard de Chardin, *Heart of Matter*, 17.
6. Teilhard de Chardin, *Heart of Matter*, 15.
7. Teilhard de Chardin, *Milieu Divin*, 78.
8. Teilhard de Chardin, *Heart of Matter*, 50.
9. Pierre Teilhard de Chardin, *Christianity and Evolution* (London: Collins, 1971), 93.
10. Pierre Teilhard de Chardin, *The Prayer of the Universe* (London: Collins, 1977), 103–104.
11. Ursula King, *Spirit of Fire: The Life and Vision of Teilhard de Chardin* (Maryknoll, NY: Orbis Books, 1996), 124.
12. Teilhard de Chardin, *Heart of Matter*, 53.
13. Teilhard de Chardin, *Christianity and Evolution*, 128.
14. Teilhard de Chardin, *Milieu Divin*, 131.

15. Teilhard de Chardin, *Milieu Divin*, 110–11.

16. King, *Spirit of Fire*, 107.

17. King, *Spirit of Fire*, 94.

18. Teilhard de Chardin, *Heart of Matter*, 117–18.

19. Teilhard de Chardin, *Prayer of the Universe*, 143, 148.

20. Pierre Teilhard de Chardin, *Toward the Future* (New York: Harcourt, 1975), 70.

21. King, *Spirit of Fire*, 18.

22. King, *Spirit of Fire*, 151.

23. Teilhard de Chardin, *Prayer of the Universe*, 133.

24. Pierre Teilhard de Chardin, *The Phenomenon of Man* (New York: Harper, 1959), 265.

25. Teilhard de Chardin, *Heart of Matter*, 50.

26. Teilhard de Chardin, *Heart of Matter*, 136.

27. Teilhard de Chardin, *Toward the Future*, 87.

28. King, *Spirit of Fire*, 148.

29. Teilhard de Chardin, *Christianity and Evolution*, 216.

30. Teilhard de Chardin, *Prayer of the Universe*, 72.

31. Teilhard de Chardin, *Milieu Divin*, 93.

32. Teilhard de Chardin, *Milieu Divin*, 146.

33. Teilhard de Chardin, *Prayer of the Universe*, 135.

34. Teilhard de Chardin, *Prayer of the Universe*, 86.

35. "Pierre Teilhard de Chardin," *Wikipedia*, https://en.wikipedia.org/wiki/Pierre_Teilhard_de_Chardin.

36. Teilhard de Chardin, *Toward the Future*, 82.

37. Teilhard de Chardin, *Christianity and Evolution*, 94–95.

38. Teilhard de Chardin, *Milieu Divin*, 154.

CHAPTER 8: SACRED COMPASSION: GEORGE MACLEOD

1. See Ron Ferguson, *George MacLeod: Founder of the Iona Community* (London: Collins, 1990).

2. George F. MacLeod, *The Whole Earth Shall Cry Glory: Iona Prayers* (Glasgow: Wild Goose, 1985), 11.

3. MacLeod, *Whole Earth Shall Cry Glory*, 16–17.

4. Ron Ferguson, ed., *Daily Readings with George MacLeod* (London: Fount, 1991), 27.

5. Ferguson, ed., *Daily Readings*, 68.

6. MacLeod, *Whole Earth Shall Cry Glory*, 13–14.

7. Ferguson, ed., *Daily Readings*, 61.

8. Ferguson, ed., *Daily Readings*, 63.

9. Ferguson, ed., *Daily Readings*, 18.

10. Ferguson, ed., *Daily Readings*, 57

11. Ferguson, ed., *Daily Readings*, 103–4.

12. Ferguson, ed., *Daily Readings*, 36–37.

13. Ferguson, ed., *Daily Readings*, 54–55.

14. Ferguson, ed., *Daily Readings*, 90.

15. MacLeod, *Whole Earth Shall Cry Glory*, 8.

16. MacLeod, *Whole Earth Shall Cry Glory*, 45.

17. Ferguson, ed., *Daily Readings*, 68–69.

18. Ferguson, ed., *Daily Readings*, 81–83.

19. Ferguson, ed., *Daily Readings*, 71.

20. MacLeod, *Whole Earth Shall Cry Glory*, 39–40.

21. MacLeod, *Whole Earth Shall Cry Glory*, 60.

CHAPTER 9: SACRED JOURNEY: KENNETH WHITE

1. Kenneth White, *Handbook for the Diamond Country: Collected Shorter Poems* (Edinburgh: Mainstream, 1990), 77.

2. White, *Handbook for the Diamond Country*, 41.

3. White, *Handbook for the Diamond Country*, 52.

4. Kenneth White, *The Bird Path: Collected Longer Poems* (Edinburgh: Mainstream, 1989), 50.

5. White, *Bird Path*, front cover leaf.

6. White, *Bird Path*, 95, 38.

7. White, *Bird Path*, 95.

8. White, *Bird Path*, 139.

9. Kenneth White, *The Blue Road* (Edinburgh: Mainstream, 1990), 127.

10. Tony McManus, *The Radical Field: Kenneth White and Geopoetics* (Dingwall: Sandstone, 2007), 32.

11. White, *Handbook for the Diamond Country*, 23.

12. Kenneth White, *Pilgrim of the Void* (Edinburgh: Mainstream, 1992), 210.

13. White, *Bird Path*, 118.

14. White, *Bird Path*, 209.

15. White, *Bird Path*, 124–25.

16. McManus, *Radical Field*, 8.

17. White, *Handbook for the Diamond Country*, 155.

18. White, *Bird Path*, 104.

19. White, *Bird Path*, 100.

20. White, *Bird Path*, 145.

21. White, *Bird Path*, 146, 141

22. White, *Bird Path*, 145.

23. White, *Bird Path*, 157–60.

24. McManus, *Radical Field*, 183.

25. McManus, *Radical Field*, 88.

26. White, *Bird Path*, 106.

27. McManus, *Radical Field*, 38.

28. McManus, *Radical Field*, 175.

29. White, *Handbook for the Diamond Country*, 50.

30. White, *Bird Path*, 106–9.

31. White, *Bird Path*, 77.

32. White, *Pilgrim of the Void*, 15.

33. McManus, *Radical Field*, 24.

34. White, *Bird Path*, 234.

35. McManus, *Radical Field*, 160.

36. White, *Bird Path*, 188–93.

37. White, *Bird Path*, 181.

38. White, *Bird Path*, 183–86.

39. White, *Bird Path*, 124.

40. White, *Bird Path*, 187.

41. White, *Bird Path*, 233–34.

42. White, *Bird Path*, 187.

Conclusion

1. See Nan Shepherd, *The Living Mountain: A Celebration of the Cairngorm Mountains of Scotland* (Edinburgh: Canongate, 2011).

THE AUTHOR

John Philip Newell is a Celtic teacher and author of spirituality who calls the modern world to reawaken to the sacredness of the earth and every human being. He resides in Edinburgh and teaches on both sides of the Atlantic. His School of Earth and Soul (A Celtic Initiative of Study, Spiritual Practice, and Compassion) offers teaching events and retreats across the United States and Canada. He also leads international pilgrimage weeks every year on the holy island of Iona in the Western Isles of Scotland. For more information about the author, visit his website at www.earthandsoul.org.